FLY FISHING FOR BONEFISH, PERMIT & TARPON

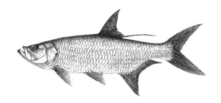

LEFTY KREH

THE LYONS PRESS
Guilford, Connecticut
An imprint of The Globe Pequot Press

The Lyons Press is an imprint of The Globe Pequot Press.

10 9 8 7 6 5 4 3 2 1

Manufactured in the United States of America
ISBN: 1-58574-604-5

The Library of Congress Cataloguing-in-Publication Data is available on file.

CONTENTS

INTRODUCTION

This book is about the three great saltwater trophy species — bonefish, permit, and tarpon. God answered the fly fisherman's prayer when he created these magnificent fish and the tropical flats in which they swim.

The world of the tropical flats is perhaps the most exciting fly-fishing water on the planet, and certainly the most fascinating saltwater environment to man. Because while the earth's vast and deep blue-water oceans remain relatively unexplored and a mystery to man — limited as our vision is to mostly nothing more than an uninformative peek just below the surface of the waves — the saltwater flats are shallow and clear, sometimes air-clear, allowing us to see and explore everything that exists in the flats' environment, from top to bottom.

This exploration can reveal a host of truly bewitching things. The sea cucumber, for example, a blackish looking slug that filters water as it lies on the bottom, is now being dissected and analyzed by scientists to determine what toxins and other matter in local waters have been trapped in its body. Or look down at the little mounds that frequently dot the floor of a flat. They may seem to be deserted, but pole across the flat at night and you'll see some of the strangest worms you could ever imagine extended from these holes, feeding.

Sunlight penetrates all the way to the bottom of salt-water flats, creating probably the richest of all our marine environments. Many species of fish and other marine creatures — hundreds or perhaps even thousands — live on the flats. Everything from microscopic creatures to giant tarpon exist side by side in this shallow water world. That's why, even when the fishing is slow, to the experienced observer the flats can be an enjoyable marine theater where there's always a super show going on.

Many fly fishermen coming to flats for the first time do not fully appreciate the effect of water temperature on their fishing prospects. Water temperature in the open sea for the most part is rather stable and subject to slow changes. Though even in deep blue water, the temperature of the water can influence gamefish behavior. Bluefish along the northeastern coast of the Atlantic Ocean, for example, only appear in the spring and summer, when water temperatures begin to reach the high 60-degree range. But they will retreat and disappear from view each fall when the water temperatures decrease.

On the flats, water temperature is a critical factor, and one that can change quite rapidly. A cold front, for example, can produce a severe drop in temperature in a matter of just a few hours, causing all the fish to rapidly depart the flats for deep water.

Consequently, usually the flats that are adjacent to deep water will have fish on them more consistently than those located on the more shallow flats well away from the ocean, both during the heat of summer and the colder periods in winter. The reason for this is that a deep body of water like the ocean is not nearly as subject to a quick change of temperature (either heating up rapidly in the summer or cooling rapidly during cold fronts) as is a shallow flat. Thus, in the winter when a cold front lowers temperatures on the flats near deep water, the next incoming tide brings in water that hasn't been so chilled; and in the summer, fresh flows of cooler water from the depths of the ocean keep these adjacent flats cooler. So in both seasons, fish tend to feed more — and therefore produce better fly-fishing action — on flats adjacent to deep water than they do on shallow flats located some distance away.

Flats can be fly fished by wading or from the deck of a flats' boat, either through poling, using an electric motor, or just drifting with the tidal current or sea breeze. Flats fishing is very comfortable in comparison to offshore fishing, since on the flats you won't be forced to brace yourself for rolling waves or put up with the smell of diesel fumes. That's why I have found that anglers who have fished offshore almost exclusively during their younger years will usually spend most of their later angling years on the flats. Except for certain bonefish habitats — like Christmas Island or Los Roques, for example, where it may be necessary to wade for the entire day — flats fishing is relatively easy and not too physically demanding. Certainly there are no mountain trails or boulders or slippery rocks to deal with. And for me and most of my fly-fishing friends, the exciting visual world of the flats and its marine creatures is so much more interesting than simply sitting in the back of an offshore cruiser for hour after hour just looking at trolled bait!

We all recognize that much of offshore fishing is blind fishing. Generally it is only when the offshore quarry comes to within a few feet of the surface that you ever see it. But when you are fly fishing on the flats, you are moving in an almost totally visual world. That's why one of the most endearing aspects of fly fishing for our three great trophy flats' fish is that it is akin to the considerable thrills associated with the sport of hunting, where it is

absolutely necessary to obtain a good visual fix on your target before you can take action by taking aim and pulling the trigger — the fly-fishing equivalent of casting and presenting the fly.

But that visual component works for the fish too. Because bonefish, permit, and tarpon are feeding in shallow water, they instinctively know they are vulnerable and, as a result, become much more alert than fish in the open sea. With offshore fly fishing, a spoiled cast to a dolphin usually results in your just having to make another cast, since the fish is usually not alarmed. That's not so on the flats, where there is a right and wrong time to make the cast. And when you make it, it has to be right on. Gean Snow, an angling friend who manages one of the most successful fly shops in the country, Angler's Inn, in Salt Lake City, calls this right moment the "window of opportunity." I can't think of a better expression to describe that brief period on saltwater when the angler must get the fly to the fish.

The greatest problem that novice fly fishermen face when they begin their flats-fishing experience is their lack of understanding of this visual world of the flats and how it affects the behavior of saltwater fish. A bass or trout angler can locate a fish, study it at his leisure, sample the water, examine what insects are drifting in or on it, and then select a fly to match the drifting creatures — a procedure that can take five minutes or more — before having finally to determine if it will be best to offer the fish a surface or an underwater fly. No such luxury of time exists on the flats. Every creature on the bright and highly visual environment of a saltwater flat is keenly aware that it has the potential at any second of its life to be bait for a

◄ *Casters enjoy a picturesque sunset.*

larger fish. It thus lives in a panic situation most of the time. At the slightest hint of danger, it will flee to deeper water. Even a six-foot tarpon might spook if a #3/0 fly only three inches long is dropped too close to it.

This behavior presents what I think is the greatest hurdle faced by freshwater anglers new to the flats: they don't understand that *speed and accuracy of the cast are vital to success in saltwater fly fishing*. In many situations the angler has a total of less than five seconds — *five seconds!* — to decide where his fly must land, make his cast, and complete his presentation. We'll be discussing that problem in the following pages, along with a number of bits and pieces of knowledge that I have been able to acquire in fly fishing for bonefish, permit, and tarpon over the last 30 years. I hope this material will be of value to you.

* * * *

No fly fisherman ever forgets the first time he hooks a large tarpon. Small ones, 30 pounds or less, certainly make an impression. But, the big ones, especially those weighing 80 pounds and larger, really do something to the angler's mind.

First there is the appearance of the fish. The guide excitedly whispers that tarpon are coming at 11 o'clock. "Be calm," you say to yourself as you look in that direction. At first there is nothing, then several backs roll and break the surface as the fish move toward you. Your heart picks up the beat and you feel warmer. "Be calm," you say to yourself. But how in the hell can you be calm when such monsters are approaching?

Then all your poise is shattered, for you can now see clearly at 50 feet how huge these fish are. Across the eyes the span is longer than some trout you have caught!

The fish give you no respite as they move swiftly forward. Without realizing it, you have aerialized the fly line and are casting worse than you can ever remember. You know the guide is giving you instructions, but either you can't hear him or you are transfixed by the big, green torpedoes that are nearly at the boat.

The line drops in front of the fish, and Almighty God! You see one of the fish rise, suck in the fly, and you dimly hear the guide yelling to strike. You drive the hook home, and then all hell breaks loose. In front of you the skin of the water is shattered, and rising out of it, whipping back and forth, is a monster fish. Water is spraying as if a fire hose has broken and you can hear the tarpon's gill covers clapping together loudly.

Suddenly the fly is thrown free and the fish crashes back to the surface. The guide fumes, "Damn it! Didn't you hear me tell you to bow?"

Hell no, you didn't hear him. For that brief span of time only you and that tarpon existed. The guide could have used a megaphone and you wouldn't have heard him.

For years you pursue the mighty tarpon, thinking it is the finest of all saltwater fly-fishing species. But then later you try for bonefish, and your perception changes — particularly when you seek the big ones.

Trying to catch big bonefish is different. But why should a fly fisherman get excited about a fish so small that a giant tarpon could eat it?

Well, I know only one experienced tarpon/bonefisherman who has said to me he would rather fish for tarpon. All others admit that bonefishing requires more skill and is more challenging. Certainly, they enjoy fishing for both species. But most experienced fishermen agree that the technical aspects of fly fishing for tarpon — the color of the fly or the pattern, for example — are really not too important. What is important in tarpon success is making a good presentation. If that is accomplished, the fish will probably take your fly.

But that's not true with bonefishing. There are so many little things you have to do correctly to get the fish to accept your offering. And, there are also so many things you can do wrong that will cause you to fail. I know of no situation in fly fishing where so many things have to be done correctly, if you expect a high rate of success.

A magazine editor once asked me if I would write a story explaining if I had one day left to fish, what species would I go for. "Think about it and call me back in a few days," he said.

I answered immediately, "I don't have to think about it, I'd go bonefishing."

For some years after I started fishing for them in the early 1960s, I figured if I hooked one bonefish out of 50 that I presented a fly to, I was lucky. Slowly that ratio diminished. Now, if I don't get one out of three bonefish to take my offering, I wonder what I'm doing wrong. It has been a long and very satisfying journey I have traveled to get me to this point. For now, nothing I do in fly fishing gives me so much pleasure as making the approach to a big bonefish, offering it a fly, and then getting a hook-up.

Permit are different, too. I landed my first permit on a fly in the late 1960s. I was so excited that I actually kissed that fish! Over the next few years I landed three more, but that was the result of untold numbers of casts with a huge variety of flies. Now, all of that has changed. In the last decade we have learned much more about catching permit, and my toll has rapidly increased.

But, permit remain perhaps the most difficult saltwater fish to take on a fly. For one thing, they usually don't swim slowly. Instead, they suddenly appear, move through the area, and are gone. There are rare occasions when you can find permit tailing. But, most of the time the fish are on the move and you have little time to decide what to do — and then to do it quickly and precisely!

Because we are still learning about catching these wary fish, and because they are not nearly as plentiful as bonefish or tarpon, there is an immense satisfaction when you ultimately land one.

So now let's enter the visual world of the saltwater flats, the world of the bonefish, permit, and tarpon. Let's begin first with a brief summary of the natural history and behavior of our three great trophy saltwater flats' fish that the late Harry Middleton prepared for us.

OVERLEAF: *Fly fishermen on the flats at Christmas Island.*

A BRIEF NATURAL HISTORY OF BONEFISH, PERMIT AND TARPON

by Harry Middleton

BONEFISH

The flats are a topography of intensities, of sunlight and shadow, of vitreous blue-green water, sizzling tropical heat, and motion. Everything moves, trembles, sways, shudders, responds to the primordial rhythms of the tides. Among the flats' undulating shadows are those of fish — among them rays and sharks, permit and tarpon, snook, sea trout, snapper, jacks, barracuda — and of particular interest to the fly fisherman — bonefish (*Albula vulpes*).

Bonefish, perhaps the ultimate fish of the saltwater flats, are creatures that sometimes seem to be ghost lights, chameleons of light. Over beds of bright sand, they are albino white, flashing like the sand itself, as hidden as a single drop of rain in a rainstorm. Over mats of turtle grass they are just another soft green shadow, given away only by their black eyes, their pattern of dark spots and stripes, their inky lateral line, the shudder at the surface above them that anglers know as nervous water.

Bonefish are survivors. Indeed, the species that still thrive in the Atlantic and Pacific are the only surviving members of its genus, in the family Albulidae. Bonefish are among the most primitive of fish, a legacy of the first bony fishes that moved through the deep blue seas of the Cretaceous period more than 115 million years ago.

The home waters of the Atlantic bonefish are the deep, warm waters south of the Carolina coast to the tropical waters off Brazil. Pacific bonefish range more widely and tolerate a great diversity of water, including the colder waters off the northern California coasts. Pacific bonefish move freely from above San Francisco, down through the warming waters off Baja, Mexico, to the deep blue-green seas off the coast of Peru. Despite this apparently broad range, the majority of bonefish populations are found in the world's warm, tropical seas, from Florida, Mexico, Central and South America to the Bahamas, off the coast of West Africa, at Christmas Island and the other coral atolls of the South Pacific basin, and Hawaii, where there are no flats and where huge bonefish live out their lives in the deep, warm blue sea. In the central Caribbean, bonefish are called *macabi,* while along the South American coast they are known as *raton* — ratfish — so named, perhaps, because of the bonefish's ability to take a native angler's bait without touching his hook.

Bonefish are characterized by a sleek and slender body, one that is a blend of grace and speed and efficiency. The head, like that of the permit, is large and blunt, sloping down to an elongated snout. The eyes are small and ink-black. The caudal fin is unevenly forked, with the upper lobe longer than the lower. All the fins are marked by soft, dark rays, from as few as 12 to 15 to as many as 19 or 20 on the dorsal fin.

Like all the great fish of the flats, bonefish are never one color. Rather, they seem to be able to change color, blending in with the changing mix of sunlight and shadow on the flats. Depending on time of day, the intensity of sunlight, clouds, and the amount of light being reflected off the water, bonefish can flash either pale blue, especially on the back, or polished silver. In shallow water in direct sun, they can also appear to be nothing more than a glow of white light marked by the dark eye, the dark bars that mark the top half of their flanks, and their darker dorsal and caudal fins. Young bonefish will have dark spots along the back rather than the distinctive bands. As the fish grows, the spots will join, giving the fish a marked pattern of darker bars or bands, usually extending down from the back to the lateral line and no farther. On an adult bonefish, this pattern of crossbars gives way to the typical dark streaks found on bigger fish.

Among bonefish, the question of size is often relative. Truly big fish can weigh as much as 20 pounds. Smaller bonefish are much more common. On the flats of Florida and Bermuda and south through the Caribbean, smaller fish, fish weighing from two to six pounds, are far more common, with bigger bonefish going from eight to as much as 15 pounds.

Bonefish have an extremely complex life cycle. Like tarpon, young bonefish go through a fascinating larval stage during which they resemble eels more than fish. However, beyond this larval stage, little is known about the bonefish's spawning habits, behavior, and deep-water movements. Bonefish are, in many ways, even more mysterious than permit. Like permit, they apparently spawn actively for as long as six to eight months, with the peak of their spawning runs coming, perhaps, in the spring.

Great schools of bonefish, thick as floating mats of menhaden, are often seen in the waters near Bermuda, in deep bays or just beyond the barrier reefs. Curiously, these large schools of bonefish often include both immature and mature fish, giving rise to speculation that the existence of these schools is a requisite part of some arcane spawning or pre-spawning ritual.

Once the eel-like young bonefish reaches a length of about two inches, or slightly larger, it begins its wondrous transition into its adult form. The larval, eel-shaped fish suddenly begins to shrink, develop fins, and transform into the sleek grace of a mature fish. As metamorphoses go, that of the bonefish is no less dramatic than that of a caterpillar into a butterfly.

Adult bonefish spend their lives moving in and out of deep water. Many may never move onto saltwater flats. Those that do follow tides onto the flats do so because of the abundant prey that is found there, the flats' bounty of water rich in shrimp and mollusks, crabs, squid, sea worms, and smaller fish. Once they are on the flats, bonefish are usually snout-down, bottom feeding, coming up onto the flat during a flooding tide, dropping off slowly on the ebbing tide.

From an angling standpoint, there are no fish on the flats that are easy. There are only challenges of differing degrees of difficulty, bonefish being among the most difficult species to stalk and capture. Bonefish are wary and suspicious, shy, and yet, once hooked, they are among the

Angler releasing a bonefish, Christmas Island. ➤

most tenacious fish in the sea, creatures of deep and uncorrupted spirit, the essence of wildness. Bonefish share something in common with brown trout: neither are ever completely off their guard. Both are alert, dyspeptic, forever cautious. If the mere shadow cast by a shore bird will send them fleeing for the safety of deep water, it takes little imagination to predict the fish's reaction to the sudden shadow of a drifting skiff, the slap of a fly line on the water, or the plop of a poorly presented fly. The border between what will attract a bonefish and what will spook it is microscopic. And what spooks one bonefish will spook every bonefish on the flat. Capturing a bonefish on a fly then becomes a matter first of avoiding its close attention, and then of tempting its rapacious hunger.

Bonefish can be stalked only if they can be found. In the extremes of most saltwater flats, with their harsh sunlight and wind, concentration becomes all important. An angler must learn to look not at the water, but through it, learning the bottom, the shape and movements of squid and rays, sharks and boxfish, crabs and shrimp, turtle grass and shifting sand. Knowing what is natural to the flat makes it a little easier to pick up a milling bonefish or the sudden appearance of something that is an anomaly, like the thin sickle silhouette of the back, tail, or fin of a tailing fish. The experienced bonefisher suspects every wrinkle of nervous water, every disturbance of mud, silt, sand. It could be a bonefish. And if the fates are kind, it could be the presence of not one bonefish but a small school, all of them preoccupied, momentarily unaware.

PERMIT

For many saltwater fly fishermen the ultimate trophy is not a seven-foot sailfish, a 40-pound striper, or a giant tarpon. No, it is the much smaller permit (*Trachinotus falcatus*), a fish that rarely exceeds 40 pounds — and many fly fishermen are delighted to catch one weighing less than 10 pounds. For these anglers, the permit is the most challenging and haunting fish of the saltwater flats, a fish so elusive that the mere sight of one is cause for celebration and piscatorial tall tales. It is not so much that permit are rare, it is that they are so often beyond temptation and therefore completely perplexing, beyond any of saltwater fly fishing's fixed rules and definitions. Permit can be among the most frustrating and difficult of all the fish we seek with a fly rod, and successful angling for them requires superb execution of all aspects of the angler's fly-fishing technique.

The Atlantic permit is often also called the great pompano. Even so, it is not related to the small pompano common to the waters off Florida. It is, however, a close relative of the Pacific permit.

Far more is known about the western Atlantic permit than its Pacific cousin. But even so, the comings and goings of permit, their behavior and lifestyle, remain a mystery. The permit is a great fish that has kept its secrets well from ichthyologists who can only theorize and surmise about its behavior. The Atlantic permit ranges widely, and can be found from the temperate waters off Brazil to the colder waters off the coast of the northeastern United States. It is difficult to estimate permit populations because the fish is so furtive. This much seems certain — that the majority of western Atlantic permit populations seem thicker near the middle of this range, in the tropical waters off the Caribbean, especially in and around Florida and east along the Gulf Stream to Bermuda.

Unquestionably the finest trophy permit fishing is to be found in the Florida Keys. Big permit can be taken from the Biscayne Bay area near Miami, and to the west of Key West, where some of the very cream of this fishing exists. In the Keys, on almost any given day, an experienced permit fisherman with the right guide can spot fish that exceed 25 or 30 pounds. Lefty tells me that one day in 1968, he spotted a pair of permit swimming off the southwest corner of the Marquesas Keys, each of which he honestly thinks exceeded 80 pounds!

It is generally believed that permit have a long spawning period, one lasting from winter through the summer, with the peak month perhaps being May or June. Since large numbers of young are frequently seen throughout the reaches of the Florida Current and the warm Caribbean waters of the Gulf Stream, it is again believed that the warm water regions of these currents may be the permit's favorite or most intensely used spawning ground.

The permit is essentially a fish of the flats and shallows. They can be found concentrated around ocean wrecks, especially during the spring when they are thought to go into deep water to spawn. But such fish are not highly regarded as a fly-fishing prize. Perhaps this is because of their schooling behavior in deep water, for when an ocean-going group of permit sees a fly, each eagerly tries

24

to out-rush the other to grab it. For whatever the reason, a wreck-caught permit is not considered to be, in any way, in a class with one caught on the flats.

As they finally take shape in the dark shadows and intense sunlight of the flats, permit are unlike any of the other flats' fish. They seem as heavy and substantial as a manhole cover. Adult permit can be truly significant fish.

The dorsal fin of the Atlantic permit is marked by six spines, while the second often has but one spine and from 16 to 21 diaphanous rays. The anal fin is marked by two detached spines and as many as 20 of the soft rays. Unlike bonefish, permit have no black spot or bar markings, and therefore their great, nearly flat surface offers little that will break the translucent character of most flats and present the angler with a distinct pattern of shape and color to search for.

The most distinctive trait of the permit is surely its unmistakable green-blue parabolic shape. Among smaller permits, the long, slender lobes of the dorsal and anal fins serve to give the permit a swept-back look. This trait is less noticeable in larger permit, since as they grow, their great, flounder-like width gives them the aspect of a finned torpedo.

Permit that spend a portion of their lives on saltwater flats seem to have a bewildering translucent color pattern. The adults, especially, can appear to have been hammered out of pure sunlight. Young permit are darker than the adult fish, often appearing either completely shadow-black or completely silver, the color of quicksilver. The coloring of the adult permit is far more subtle, bewildering. Under a cloudless flats' sky, when seen at all, the fish appears completely pellucid, a chimera of light and shadow. In shadow, or once clearly seen, permit are pale blue or ash gray on their wide, powerful backs, and burnished silver on their deep flanks and rounded bellies. Permit that have yet to reach full size can also be marked by a unique dim blood-red cast or glow, a trait that is totally absent from big permit. Big permit, say above 15 or 20 pounds, are almost always a stunning silver with smudges of mixed greens and blues. Other important color marks found on big permit are the nearly always shadow-colored fins. Often the pelvic and anal fins will be colored burnt orange.

While large numbers of permit are never caught, there are always many sightings. Like bonefish, they tend to keep to deep water, coming up onto the flats on spring tides, in small schools of five to 10 fish, while bigger fish frequently travel and feed alone. From an angling standpoint, it is important to remember that permit, because they are big fish, need deeper water than bonefish. Rarely will you find a big permit on a shallow flat. Their penchant for deep-water flats makes seeing them even more difficult. Permit are bottom feeders, but unlike bonefish, they seldom create muds or clouds of silt as they feed. Nervous water, tailing fish, and distinctive dark fins are what most often give the permit away to the angler.

Finding permit is often difficult. Once found, though, they can give even the most accomplished fly fisherman the challenge of his angling life. Permit will take a fly, but getting them to do so is never easy. And once hooked, the permit's spirit has no limit: it can run as fast as a bonefish and it will run, at that speed, again and again, running for deep water, wrenching and twisting as it runs, banging its blunt, wide head hard on the bottom in an effort to throw the hook, break the line.

For many anglers there is no greater experience than taking a permit on the fly, and for some, fly fishing for permit can become the obsession of a lifetime.

TARPON

Tarpon (*Megalops atlantica*) are among the most pursued and most beloved of all the saltwater fish. Primarily it is a fish found where freshwater and saltwater mix, especially in the waters of south Florida in estuaries, the mouths of freshwater rivers, inlets, and channels.

Its range is far more compact than that of either the permit or bonefish. Tarpon are found on both sides of the Atlantic. In the western Atlantic, tarpon have been found, though rarely, as far north as Nova Scotia, and as far south as the tropical waters off the coast of Brazil. But they are most plentiful in the waters around Florida and the Bahamas, down to the waters off southern Mexico. Along the eastern edge of the Atlantic, tarpon are found along the African coast from Senegal south.

Like bonefish, tarpon are truly ancient fish, belonging to the Elopidae family of bony fishes. Evolution has created with the tarpon a deeply beautiful and distinctive fish. Among its most telling characteristics are its nearly straight line from head to tail, a line that gives its massive head an almost exaggerated blunt look. Just behind the massive mouth and head, the back of a big, mature tarpon is gently arched. Its great orange eyes are set high on the dorsal side of the head. Tarpon possess a massive mouth, with the bottom jaw projecting out beyond the head and nearly always held slightly agape, giving the fish a pugnacious look. Fully open, the mouth takes on the aspect of a bucket. The dorsal fin is high on the back and well off center. It is grayish in color and rayed, with the last of its 11 to 16 rays becoming an elongated tailing lobe or spike. The tail is forked and deep gray to black in color. Like the dorsal fin, the anal fin is marked by 20 to 25 soft rays. The last ray, especially among mature tarpon, while not a separate lobe, is definitely spiked.

Perhaps the most telling physical aspect of the tarpon, other than its great flat head and enormous mouth, is its scales, which are so thick and heavy that they look like links of polished armor plate. Because of these scales and the way sunlight is reflected off them, giving the appearance of hammered silver, tarpon are also called silverfish or silver kings. This brilliant silver is easily the fish's most dominant color, though it too can change — in shading at least — as water and weather conditions change, ranging from sunburst silver to a dull silver pewter. Often, the backs of tarpon will look soft blue, especially as they roll on the surface of the water. Too, the combination of sunlight and shadow and clouds can give their fins and tail a beautiful green-blue color. The belly of a tarpon is always as stark as platinum.

Tarpon are less mercurial and more plentiful than either bonefish or permit. Often, their numbers can be staggering. During spawning, a single mature, fertile female may carry as many as 10 million eggs. Peak spawning months for tarpon are from May into early autumn. There is usually little activity past the end of September. In Florida, the top tarpon months are usually May, June, and July, though many big tarpon have been taken in the Florida Keys as late as January. Tarpon spawn — at least in Florida — in estuaries and in the mouths of larger rivers. Tarpon can tolerate both salt and freshwater.

Indeed, they are often found beyond the salt or brackish water zones, higher up rivers in undiluted freshwater.

Tarpon, like bonefish, go through an eel-like larval stage. Those that survive can become incredibly big fish indeed. While small tarpon are usually designated as fish weighing between 10 and 20 pounds, adult specimens can be eight feet long and weigh more than 300 pounds. Tarpon grow slowly throughout their lives. Those who live to grow to 100 pounds are usually 12 to 17 years of age, ancient for a fish. Young, small tarpon are more common in brackish streams and rivers. While bigger tarpon seem to prefer water with less salt, such as the deeper waters of inlets, bays, estuaries, larger channels, and river mouths. Both young and old tarpon are commonly found in the shallow lakes of the mangrove flats.

Tarpon are carnivorous and tireless hunters, always on the prowl for small prey, especially mullet, blue crabs, and catfish. Tarpon can often be seen rolling on the surface. This is not always an activity associated with feeding. Because tarpon have a gas bladder, or false lung, which allows them to survive in water low in oxygen, rolling tarpon may simply be breathing, emptying and filling their air bladder, rather than feeding. It is nearly impossible to tell. For the angler, it is always best to assume that a rolling tarpon is feeding and cast to it. For even if the tarpon is not feeding, if the temptation is great enough, it will certainly strike.

One of the most popular gamefish, not just among saltwater fly fishermen, but among all saltwater fishermen, tarpon are stalked in any number of ways. Drift fishing is particularly popular among hardware fishermen, using baits of mullet, crabs, or shrimp. For those who have had the experience, though, and especially among those who have actually boated one of these incredible fish, no other angling experience can match the thrill of taking a tarpon on a fly rod. Fly fishermen who have hooked a tarpon, fought it well, brought it to the boat, and released it, will tell you earnestly that the experience is the most fun an angler can have with his clothes on.

Stalking tarpon in Florida waters with a fly rod is usually done by sight casting to fish along the banks of a channel, estuary, or mouth of a river, or to groups or pods of fish cruising or feeding on the flats. In the early summer, when tarpon are on the move, the fortunate angler might jump as many as three to seven fish a day. Oftentimes, especially on the flats, small tarpon may be feeding in very large numbers, allowing the skilled fly fisherman to jump a truly staggering number of fish in a day. In fact, many fly fishermen prefer fishing for small tarpon, because they would rather have a chance at filling their day with many fish than concentrating on only one great fish that might require a very long time to boat, exhausting both angler and fish.

Of all the fish on the flats, one thing above all is certain about tarpon of any size: they are all extremely difficult to hook. Tarpon, even the big ones, do not attack the fly as savagely as most saltwater species. Indeed, many a tarpon is lost simply because anglers miss the strike, or strike too late, as the tarpon strike can be deceptively soft, no more than a slight tug or a tenuous bump. Caught up in the excitement of a likely strike, the sight of a tarpon sucking in a fly, its great mouth wide, bucket-wide and bucket-deep, many anglers pull the trigger too quickly and simply jerk the fly out of the fish's gaping mouth. And given the rough texture of its jaws, mouth, and throat, setting the hook on a tarpon has to be done with strength and power. There is no way that fly fishing for tarpon can be described as a delicate sport.

Once hooked, a tarpon loses almost none of its advantage. Big tarpon are so massive and powerful that they have been known to tow skiffs off the flats and far out into deep water. In such circumstances, invariably, the longer the fight, the greater the chances that the fish and not the angler will succeed.

Harry Middleton was the author of several distinguished books on fly fishing and the fly-fishing life, three of which, The Earth is Enough, On the Spine of Time, *and* Into That Bright Country *(all published by Simon & Schuster), have, in the opinion of many observers, become classics.*

OVERLEAF: *Fly fishing the flats at the Berry Islands, Bahamas.*

CHAPTER ONE

THE BASIC RULES OF THE GAME

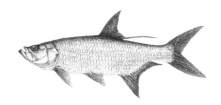

There are a number of simple but fundamental rules that should be observed when fishing for bonefish, permit, tarpon, or really, all shallow-water saltwater species.

(1) Don't cast to a bonefish, permit, or tarpon until you can see it. Blind casting usually results only in spooking the fish and losing the fishing opportunity.

(2) Don't rush. *Regardless of what the guide is saying, make your movements and cast at a speed that is comfortable for you.* Remember, the difference between rushing a cast and operating at a comfortable speed for your skill level is usually less than two or three seconds. Operating at your own pace will generally result in a better presentation.

(3) Learn to cast well. If you can't shoot, you can't hunt. If you can't cast well, then wind, distance, and the short amount of time often required to make a saltwater presentation are going to combine to result in frustration and likely failure. My deep-seated opinion on this issue — despite arguments made by some to the contrary — is that while fly fishing on the saltwater flats does not necessarily require longer casts than freshwater, *it does require better*

casts. Of all the reasons that people fail to catch fish on the flats, perhaps the inability to make a cast that will properly deliver the fly is the most important. Becoming a really good caster is absolutely necessary if you hope to become proficient at catching bonefish, permit, and tarpon.

(4) Especially with bonefish and permit, you should use the longest leader that you can handle well. The shorter the leader the more likely that you'll spook fish.

(5) Constantly check your tackle and equipment. Sharp hooks are vital if you want to hook the quarry. After hooking a fish, check the hook point for sharpness. Make sure that your line on the deck is not tangled in some obstruction. Examine your tippet for nicks or abrasions. Make sure you are not standing on your leader or line. Frequently check your leader for wind knots. If mangroves or other obstructions are nearby, make sure you have room for the back cast. Keep checking everything that can go wrong, for in flats fishing it will go wrong . . . Murphy's Law is in force on the flats.

(6) Noise is an important factor: avoid it at all costs. Wading too rapidly, for example, can alert fish. *In shallow water (less than 18 inches) fish hear people talking loudly.* Avoid yelling or talking loudly when nearby fish are moving through such a thin water column.

When working a flats' fish, the noise that may be created by the pick-up for your back cast is a critical factor, the importance of which is not fully recognized by many saltwater anglers. *You should never make a back cast near a fish until you have lifted all the line from the water, with only your leader and fly remaining under the surface.* Making a back cast while some of the fly line is still on the surface creates a noise that will alert the fish and generally cause it to flee. This is one of the most frequent mistakes made by inexperienced flats' fishermen.

And whether you're anchored, staked out, or being poled, your flats' boat may be emitting a good deal more noise than you may realize, particularly as a result of small waves lapping against the hull and sending out tiny radar-like signals to fish. If you're considering the purchase of a flats' boat, it's worth checking with owners of a similar model to determine how quiet its hull is.

(7) Knots are the weakest link in the tackle chain. Particularly in saltwater, it is vital that you understand how to tie good ones.

(8) Movement by the angler — of his body, his fly rod, or his fly line — can easily be seen by fish. That's why wading, which allows you to present a low profile and get very close to the fish, can be very effective in many flats' situations. But, whether you're wading or casting from a boat, always keep your body and rod as low as possible when approaching and making a presentation on the flats.

(9) Keep in mind that flies do not attack fish. Aside from a splashy or visible warning that may be given to the fish by a faulty presentation, *how* the fly approaches the fish is the single most important reason for a refusal. *Your fly should always be presented to the fish so that it creates the appearance of bait that is either unaware of the nearby presence of a predator, or is attempting to escape from it. Never should your fly appear to be attacking the fish!*

(10) Learn how to look for the fish you seek. Bonefish, permit, and tarpon have silvery sides which act like mirrors, reflecting back to the angler the area they are swimming over. But there are tiny indicators that we will be examining that will assist you in detecting fish.

OVERLEAF: *A display of typical bonefishing tackle.*

CHAPTER TWO

TACKLE FOR BONEFISH AND PERMIT

We will examine the tackle requirements for fly fishing for bonefish and permit together, as they are quite similar in most respects, the major difference being only that permit fishing requires slightly heavier lines and stouter rods. (Tarpon fly fishing in most instances requires an entirely different tackle set-up, so it will be treated separately.)

RODS

Bonefish are normally taken on rods that will throw lines ranging from size 4 to 11. Today, the most popular rods are made from graphite fibers, although there are also some fine fiber glass rods available. While there are people who pride themselves on fly fishing for bonefish only with a 4 to 6-weight rod, I think they are trying to prove a point with inadequate tackle. It is certainly true that on a very calm day, using small #6 or #8 flies, you can catch bonefish quite easily on a 4, 5, or 6-weight rod.

But after using such light tackle on bonefish for a considerable number of years, I have concluded that people who like to use light gear probably also like to hunt big game with a pistol. I'm sure that under special circumstances experienced hunters can kill a deer or an elk — or even an elephant, for that matter — with a pistol; but had they instead armed themselves with a rifle, they would certainly have been able to capitalize on more hunting opportunities and have bagged more game.

Even so, you may decide that you prefer to fly fish for bonefish with lighter rods and lines. I certainly have no quarrel with anyone who chooses this technique. After all, fly fishing is for fun. And if light-tackle fly fishing brings you pleasure, that's what you should use. But you should be willing to accept the reality that with light tackle you won't be able to cast as far or as well into the wind, or be able to throw the heavier flies that may be needed in certain situations, as you can with heavier tackle.

But I definitely recommend that when making your tackle selection you not go to the other end of the spectrum and choose larger 10 or 11-weight fly rods and lines for bonefish. Not only is such a rig heavy and less fun to use, it also will generally result in producing a major technique deficiency: the heavy line crashing to the surface and alerting or alarming the fish. I simply can't think of any situation in fly fishing for bonefish in which using 10 or 11-weight rods would be advisable. If the wind is blowing too hard and you have to use a rod that is heavier than a 9 weight, then it's probably not worth bonefishing at all at that time.

Of course, you could opt for a 9-weight rod, as it handles the wind pretty well, too. But again, with the heavier rod you are risking the possibility of more frequent presentation-spoiling splashdowns of the heavier line.

If there is just a little breeze, a 7-weight rod is a nice tool. It's relatively light and a pleasure to cast, and fighting a bonefish with a rod of this weight, with which you can really feel the strength and power of the fish as it makes its celebrated long surges, is obviously much more fun than anything you could experience with heavier tackle.

But as far as I am concerned, without question the best all-around rod for bonefishing is an 8 weight. Bonefish flats are almost always host to sea breezes, more often than not pretty stiff ones. Add to that the fact that so many bonefish seem to appear upwind of the angler. Therefore, for most typical days on the flats, I find an 8-weight rod to be ideal. With the proper leader it will allow you to make soft line impacts on the presentation. It can handle breezes of any reasonable velocity. And it will comfortably cast bonefish flies in the most popular sizes from #2 to #8.

However, when selecting a permit rod, you need to consider that while you still must be able to make a delicate presentation of the fly, more often than not you will be throwing a heavily weighted crab pattern to permit — unlike bonefish flies that are almost always light, delicate, and easy to cast. For that reason, my favorite rod for permit fishing is a 9 weight. It is the lightest one that will give a reasonably soft impact of the line on the surface and still have enough weight to carry crab flies to the fish.

I believe that a rod of 9 feet is the ideal length for bonefish and permit fly fishing. Longer rods are okay, but I really find no advantages to having more length than that in the rod, and shorter rods (especially shorter than 8 1/2 feet) hamper my efforts when trying to deliver the fly.

There are many fly rods on the market today. In fact, almost any rod you can buy that costs $150 or more will probably cast better than you do. Of course, the more expensive rods perform better. And if you can cast well, they help you do a better job of delivering the fly under any kind of difficult condition.

When evaluating saltwater flats' fly rods and their design, I believe there is an important but often overlooked factor that needs to be considered. That is the size of the butt or stripping guide — the largest guide on any fly rod, located closest to the handle. When a cast is made and the angler shoots line, the line coming off the water or deck does not come up to the stripping guide in a smooth wavering line. Instead, as shown in the illustration below, it approaches the guide in snarls, with coils that must be smoothed out before the line can slip through the guide. But the smaller the guide, the more the line is choked as it tries to enter. And most commercially available fly rods are equipped with a stripping guide that is simply too small to deal with this problem.

The importance of the size of this first rod guide cannot be overemphasized. I have mentioned this rod design deficiency in several of my other books in the Library, but

Shooting line is liable to become snarled in a rod equipped with a stripping guide that is too small.

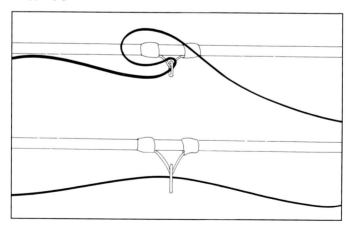

I have decided to take a bit of space and include it again in this book because it is critically important to good saltwater fly casting technique, and I want you to pay special attention to it.

On most rods offered on the market today, the standard stripping guide has a diameter of 12 mm, and some are even smaller. But my personal preference for a stripping guide on any rod casting lines from size 7 or larger is a stripping guide with a diameter of 22 mm. In my opinion, the absolute minimum size is 16 mm on any rod of this weight.

Such a larger stripping guide is especially important if you can cast a fast or long line. If you are able to cast a long, high-speed line, you have probably had the experience of shooting a swiftly moving line and having it snag or wrap around the 12-mm (or smaller) stripping guide.

This small stripping guide size creates problems on short-range casts, too. Since with bonefish and permit (and tarpon) most casts are frequently made at very short distances, as the angler is on the hunt searching for fish, he is generally retaining just a short amount of line outside his rod tip. On the cast, the balance of the line has to be pulled through the rod guides as it is shot to the target. The larger the stripping guide, the easier that short length of line outside the tip can pull line through on the shoot.

If the rod you intend to use for saltwater flats fly fishing does not possess a stripping guide in the sizes I have recommended, I strongly urge you to replace it with one in a proper size. It will make a big difference in your casting technique.

It is also important that your rod be equipped with the largest size snake guides that it can support and still cast well. It has been my experience that rods equipped with one-foot Fuji guides are not the most desirable. The feet break if bent more than once, and the distance obtained through their use does not seem to equal that of standard chrome-plated snake guides. What is important is to use the largest snake guides you can (usually referred to as size 6) throughout the tip section.

The tip-top should be a large ring. In fact, some fly fishermen equip their saltwater rods with a lightweight spinning rod tip that has a large ring. The reason for the concern for a large tip-top and large guides along the rod blank is that with a fast-running flats' fish, frequently the line is being pulled out so rapidly through the guides that a snarl or knot will be created in the line. When that happens, the larger the diameter of the guides and tip-top, the more likely the knot will be able to slip through so that a break-off can be avoided.

When selecting a fly rod for saltwater flats fishing, the butt extension of the rod — any portion of the fly rod that protrudes below the reel seat — is worth considering, as a butt extension that can be placed against the body to keep the reel a few inches away and permit easy turning of the reel handle to recover line is a favorable asset when fighting heavy or fast-running saltwater fish.

One way that a fly fisherman can achieve this kind of butt extension is by using a rod designed with a reel seat in an up-locking style, so that when the reel is positioned on the rod, the threads located at the base of the rod handle will permit the locking ring or rings to move up from the base to lock the reel. (As opposed to a down-locking design, in which the locking rings are positioned between the cork of the handle and the reel.)

On such an up-locking design, the threads on the reel seat provide the angler with a partial butt extension. Fortunately, most rods being manufactured today are equipped with this desirable up-locking reel seat design.

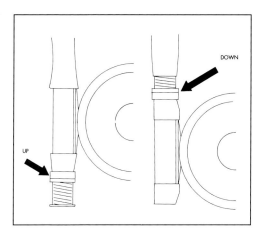

*Up and Down-
Locking Reel
Seats*

DOWN

UP

Or you can purchase a rod equipped with a butt extension. But it should be a design that does not extend more
than two inches from the end of the threads on the reel
seat. A butt extension longer than that will frequently trap
the fly line and either spoil the cast or cause a leader break
when the escaping fish comes tight against the snarled
line. I prefer no more than a one-inch butt extension on
all my saltwater fly rods. I find this is ample length
extension to hold the reel off my body and permit me to
turn the reel handle easily.

Most people who fish for bonefish, permit, and tarpon
must travel to fish. The recent development of three and
four-piece graphite travel rods by our leading rod
manufacturers has been a giant step forward in the lives
of such anglers. For not only are such rods easy to carry
on board the plane in order to avoid lost baggage problems, many are actually better casting tools than their
one or two-piece counterparts. I highly recommend them.

OVERLEAF: *Casting to bonefish at Andros Island.*

Many types of fly reels have been used for fly fishing for bonefish and permit over the years. Even some freshwater models have served pretty well. But there is the obvious disadvantage associated with using a freshwater reel constructed of materials that are not corrosion proof. Because even with the most careful use on the flats, reels are inevitably going to be exposed to saltwater — when an angler bends down to lift a fish out of the water and inadvertently soaks the reel in the sea, for example, or merely from the salt spray that will accumulate on the reel when the boat is running in a chop. Therefore, the angler should choose a reel that is designed to be resistant to the corrosive effects of saltwater. This is most commonly

The best saltwater fly reels are made from solid — but not cast — metal. Below is shown a typical reel made from solid rods of aluminum, the Billy Pate Reel.

achieved by manufacturers today by anodizing the outer metal surfaces of the reel. Flats' fishermen prefer reels that are light, too, so almost all saltwater models are made today of lightweight metals, usually aluminum.

Reels come in various sizes, depending upon how much fly line and backing they are designed to carry on the spool. You may have read about scorching runs of bonefish of 200 yards or more. Well, in 30 years of actively pursuing bonefish, and after having caught even a number of 10-pounders, I can report to you that I have never experienced a bonefish running away with more line than the length of my fly line plus 150 yards of backing. In fact, only a half dozen or so have ever taken more than 100 yards of backing.

Of course, during the excitement when a bonefish zings across the water to a distance the length of a fly line plus 100 yards of backing, it *looks and feels* like that fish has gone maybe 250 yards! But stand at one end of a football field and imagine a fish running to the other end! I would guess that the longest average run of an eight-pound bonefish (which is a pretty fair-sized bonefish in almost any part of the world) would consume only 75 yards of backing, plus the fly line.

Regarding permit, I find that when a permit is first hooked, it will make a straight, scalding-hot run but then tend to swim in large circles, which doesn't really pull a lot more line off the reel. My experience is that a 10-pound bonefish will run farther on its first frantic run than will a 20-pound permit. The permit will certainly fight a great deal harder than a bonefish, but it does its fighting relatively near the angler.

What I am suggesting is that to fish for bonefish and permit, you don't need reels with a capacity of 250 to 350 yards of backing plus fly line, as some advocate. Such reels have the major disadvantages of being much more expensive and much heavier than is required to get the job done. I enjoy fly fishing with lighter reels, those that have a capacity for holding only 180 to 200 yards of backing plus the fly line.

Despite what I have to say, if you want to enjoy the smaller, lighter reels but are not comfortable with a maximum reel capacity of fly line plus 200 yards of backing, you might follow the practice of some saltwater fly fishermen I know, which is simply to shorten the fly line by cutting off 20 feet or so of its rear portion. This will give you additional space on the spool to add considerably more backing.

The reel should have a super slick drag that doesn't surge when the fish makes its run. You may recall in an earlier book in the Library I discussed drag action: that a reel is said to have a *starting* drag and a *running* drag — starting drag simply meaning that the drag mechanism of the reel won't release line until enough pressure is applied; running drag meaning the amount of resistance needed to keep the spool in motion against the drag. In almost all reels, it will take more pressure on the line to get a drag started than it will to keep it running, just as it's much harder to get a stalled car moving than it is to keep it moving.

I suggest you keep in mind, from what I have said, that while some reels will have a very smooth running drag on a steady pull, these type reels may require much more initial pressure to initiate their starting drag, and you need to recognize the difference. For optimum performance, it's desirable to fish with a reel that has a low starting drag, one that requires little more line pressure to start the drag than it does to keep the drag running or slipping during the fish's run.

You can check the drag on your reel to see if it is performing smoothly by using the following test. Attach the end of your line to the back of a bicycle and adjust the reel drag so that a straight pull of about two pounds will allow the drag to slip. Then, have a person slowly ride away on the bike, pulling line from the reel. If the rod tip bounces up and down, that indicates that the reel is allowing the line to slip unevenly. This jerkiness may break a fragile leader if the fish runs quickly. With a well-performing drag, you ought to be able observe that the rod tip will barely bob up and down as the bicycler rides away with the line end.

In fishing for bonefish, I prefer to use my fingers on the reel and line to apply pressure and use very little drag. This reduces the chances of the fish surging against a heavier drag setting and breaking the leader. To obtain the desired drag pressure, place the line in your lips (be sure they are dry and free of lip balm) and adjust the reel drag fairly tightly. Then slowly back off on the drag adjustment until you can just pull off line while holding it clenched

Lefty demonstrates how he sets drag pressure for bonefish.

in your lips. I find that this is all the drag you will need to handle any bonefish. Remember, too, as the amount of line diminishes on the spool when the fish makes a long run, drag pressure will increase.

One of the most important factors in insuring that your reel drag will operate smoothly for many years is to be certain to release all pressure from the drag at the end of each day's fishing. Most good saltwater reels have one or more soft drag washers which under adjusted tension allow the spool to slip when enough pressure is exerted on the spool by the fish. If the reel is left with that adjusted pressure on the washers for an extended time, the compression will slowly squeeze the softness from the washers, severely hampering their performance.

The drag mechanism of the reel also needs to be maintained properly. Some manufacturers suggest rubbing a bit of neat's foot oil on the drag washers. Others recommend a variety of compounds, usually made from a silicone base. To be sure of how to maintain your drag washers, check the manual that accompanied the reel.

BACKING

On all fly reels in saltwater, fishing for all species, including bonefish and permit, I prefer 30-pound Dacron or Micron backing, rather than 12 or 20-pound. The lighter backing materials tend to fray with long use, but 30-pound backing should last for years of repeated use.

If you have doubts about the wear your backing has sustained, check it with a magnifying glass. Look at a new piece (which should be some of the line located deep on the spool) and compare it with the backing near the rear of the fly line. If the Dacron or Micron shows small spurs (something like the appearance of miniature barbed wire), it should be replaced.

LINES

There are four basic shapes of fly lines: level, double-taper, shooting-taper, and weight-forward. When seeking bonefish and permit, as far as I am concerned, you can eliminate the first three types and concentrate solely on the weight-forward design.

A weight-forward line is one in which the rear of the line is very thin compared to its forward portion. It is basically constructed in the following manner. The very front part of the line (the tip) is usually level in diameter and very short — often no more than 18 inches in length. Just back of this tip the line gradually tapers to a larger diameter (the front taper). Then there is a fairly long, fat, level section (the belly). The line then diminishes in size as it tapers back to its rear portion (the rear taper). Then finally comes a rather long portion behind the rear taper (the running line) that is almost always level in diameter.

But, there are a host of different designs that have been created in the last few years by the line manufacturers around this basic weight-forward taper design concept. The tip, the front taper, even the belly and back tapers of these designs may differ in length or diameter for various fishing purposes.

On lines that manufacturers designate as a "standard or conventional" weight-forward line, usually the heavier the line, the longer will be its belly section. A standard or conventional weight-forward 8-weight line, for example, has about a 1-foot level tip, a 6-foot front taper, approximately a 30-foot heavy belly section, and a 3 to 4-foot

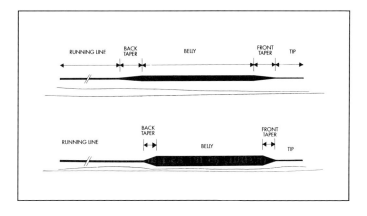

Design of Standard or Conventional Weight-Forward Line (top) *versus Bonefish Taper Line. The running line at the rear (toward the reel) is identical in both designs. In the standard or conventional design, the back and front tapers, as well as the belly, are longer. On the Bonefish Taper line, the back and front tapers are shorter. The belly is shorter and larger.*

rear taper, yielding a total length from the tip to the back of the rear taper of 40 to 41 feet. A 6-weight line would be a few feet shorter in the heavier belly section of the line.

A weight-forward 8-weight line in the configuration designated as a Bonefish Taper — a popular design which many saltwater anglers are now using — has a 1-foot tip, approximately a 4-foot front taper, a 23-foot belly section, and a 3-foot back taper, yielding a total length from the tip to the back of the rear taper of 30 to 31 feet — or about 10 feet shorter than a standard or conventional weight-forward taper. The Saltwater Taper and Bass-Bug Taper designs are very similar to that of the Bonefish Taper.

All fly lines are calibrated in reference to the weight of the first 30 feet of the line. An 8-weight line, for example, weighs 210 grains, plus or minus eight grains. Because the

Bonefish Taper is about 10 feet shorter than the standard or conventional weight-forward line, but still weighs the same, something has to be different. And so it is. The diameters of the belly of the Bonefish, Saltwater, and Bass-Bug Tapers are all much larger.

There are advantages to using a Bonefish Taper. But they can be offset by its disadvantages. Obviously, a Bonefish Taper will come to the water with a more disturbing splashdown, as its shorter front taper, heavy belly, and blunt back taper are not going to land as delicately as a conventional weight-forward line. This is an important consideration when presenting a fly to a bonefish or permit — two of the easiest species to frighten on a cast.

When fishing for bones or permit, the angler is standing either on the deck of a flats' boat or wading, with a small amount of line stripped outside the rod tip and the fly and leader held in readiness. When a fish is spotted, a hasty cast has to be made. As I have said repeatedly, the angler's ability to get into quick action is usually the key to whether the fish is going to see the fly or not, and thus whether there's going to be any action. In these circumstances, *if you are not a good fly caster, that is, if you can comfortably cast only up to 60 feet on a calm day,* then perhaps the Bonefish Taper is your best choice of lines, because the head and tapers are so short on this line that once you get a small amount of line outside the rod tip, you can generally get going and execute a hasty cast.

But in getting the fly to the fish quickly in this manner with a Bonefish Taper, keep in mind that *you may be sacrificing a quiet presentation.*

For more experienced anglers, who can cast comfortably at distances greater than 60 feet, there is another problem with a Bonefish Taper line. When a long forward cast is made, as the rod tip stops, the line — which at that point is straight behind the angler — begins to unroll at the rod tip, and continues to unroll until the leader deposits the fly on the target. With a Bonefish Taper, when you are holding a great length of line in the air behind you, you will confront a special problem. For as the rod sweeps forward and stops, the thin running line behind the rear taper is not thick enough to support the heavy belly section of the Bonefish Taper. As a result, it will tend to collapse, often spoiling the delicacy of the cast and the subsequent presentation of the fly.

Therefore, I do not recommend the Bonefish Taper design for competent casters who can routinely throw in excess of 60 feet in calm conditions. If you can throw that much line or more, then a conventional weight-forward line is a better selection, in my opinion, as it will allow you to false cast better when holding a long line in the air, and will definitely deliver the fly with a quieter presentation.

Lines come in a variety of colors from white to very dark. There is some controversy about what is the best color of line to use in fly fishing for the saltwater flats' species. I think this issue really boils down to what you personally like. On the flats, my favorite line colors are the bright ones, especially the fluorescent ones. Since I favor casting to bonefish and permit with as long a leader as I can, this long-leader length to some degree nullifies any concern I might otherwise have about my bright fluorescent fly line frightening fish.

I have suggested previously that fly fishing on the flats is particularly *a visual experience*. The advantage of using a brightly colored line is that it gives the angler a significant visual advantage in making his presentation. Because I believe that since most fishermen are able to see their fly line unrolling toward the target, they can observe its flight and have a better opportunity to control its accuracy.

If you don't believe me, you might try this trick. Look at a target as you are false casting. Then just before you make the forward cast, close your eyes. After the cast, strip in some line and false cast again with your eyes closed. Duplicate this blind casting routine several times. Then, do the same thing but with your eyes open. I think you will be surprised at how much more accurately you can cast when you are able to observe your fly line unrolling through the air toward the target.

LEADERS

The preferred leader for bonefish and permit is a tapered leader, that is, a leader constructed of several sections of monofilament, beginning with a heavy butt section (the heaviest or thickest portion attached to the fly line) connected to one or more progressively smaller sections of monofilament (the mid-section), the last portion of which is connected to the smallest and weakest section that makes up the very end of the leader (the tippet).

There are some fundamental rules for building a good basic saltwater tapered leader that will help you when fishing for bonefish, permit, and other saltwater species.

First, it's important to understand why we need to use a long tapered leader, and what are its functions. The major reason for using such a leader is to get the splashdown of the fly line on the surface of the water as far away from the fish as practical. Because it is the crash of the line falling to the water that frightens fish — not the leader.

Second, when the rod tip stops on the forward cast, the fly line begins unrolling, starting at the tip of the rod and proceeding toward the target. As all of the line unrolls, the leader, following in turn behind the line, has also to unroll properly in order to deposit the fly at the target area.

Third, whatever the size of the fly that is being pre-sented to the fish, the leader must be able to carry enough of the energy of the cast throughout the monofilament to turn it over as the line and leader unroll.

Fourth, again whatever the size of the fly being pre-sented, the size of the tapered leader's tippet is important, because if it is too stiff, it will kill the fly's natural action underwater. In most bonefishing situations, leader tippets of 10 or 12-pound test are ideal, as bonefish are not too leader shy. That is not to say that leaders cannot spook bonefish. They will spook sometimes from leaders that contrast too much with the environment. That is why experienced bonefishermen prefer leader tippets that are either clear in color or very lightly tinted. Many people, including myself, feel that dark or fluorescent-colored leaders spook fish. At Christmas Island, for example, the natives will advise all anglers not to use dark-colored leader tippets on the white sand flats.

With these fundamental rules in mind, let's look at the design of a typical tapered saltwater leader, starting first with an examination of the butt section.

Employing a butt section of stiff monofilament, with the mid-section and tippet made of a much softer monofilament, is one of those "rules of fly fishing" which is often wrong; and yet, because of tradition, has been handed down from generation to generation and con-tinues to be used without further thought. I have believed for years that such a leader design is wrong.

I am joined in this opinion by experienced anglers who concur that this is not the best way to construct a leader, particularly a bonefish or permit leader. These type leaders should be at least 10 feet long — or even longer if your casting skills and the day's wind conditions permit.

A butt section that is too stiff just doesn't perform as well as one made from what would be termed medium-stiff or medium-limp monofilament. This is because at the end of the forward cast two critical events are occurring: the line (as well as the leader) is unrolling; and the line energy that was generated by the cast is diminishing, so much so that most casters need help in getting the leader to straighten right at the end. As the line is unrolling, when the unrolling motion reaches the stiff-butt section of the leader, this rather inflexible monofilament, assisted by the loss of line energy, *resists* unrolling.

But, a leader constructed with a butt section of medium-stiff monofilament is better able to transmit the remaining casting energy through the butt section so that the leader will continue to unroll properly.

Of course, just as too stiff a monofilament in the butt section resists turning the leader over, using too limp a monofilament in the butt section will simply collapse the leader in the middle of the cast.

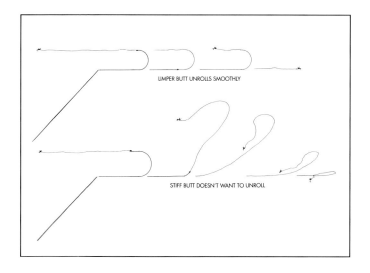

LIMPER BUTT UNROLLS SMOOTHLY

STIFF BUTT DOESN'T WANT TO UNROLL

If a monofilament that is a bit limper than what is generally called "hard monofilament" is used, a more efficient butt section is ensured. I find that the regular monofilament that is used on trolling, casting, and spinning reels — a material that is not regarded as either limp or stiff — is ideal for constructing the butt section as well as the rest of a tapered saltwater leader.

Of the many brands of medium-stiff or medium-limp monofilament available from fly shops and catalogs today, (all of which are probably just fine), there are two I have been using lately that I can recommend to you, those manufactured by Maxima and Ande.

I know this admonition against the use of heavy and stiff monofilament for the butt sections of tapered leaders flies in the face of what many experts have been claiming for years. But give it a test and I think you'll agree.

I favor building a loop on the butt section of my leader. I've been doing this for more than three decades and have never had a problem with it. A loop never hangs up in the guides, and it permits me to unloop the leader and exchange it quickly for another leader of a different weight or length — a procedure that comes in handy when conditions change abruptly, as they frequently do on the flats. There are several strong loop knot designs to choose from. I prefer the non-slip mono loop.* Or you may prefer

----

*Note: Illustrations of all knots mentioned in this book appear in the Appendix of a companion volume in the Library, *The American Masters Fly Fishing Symposium, Part Two - Tackle,* pages 158-170. Or for more detailed tying instructions, see *Practical Fishing Knots II*, by Mark Sosin and Lefty Kreh (Lyons & Burford, Publishers, 31 West 21 Street, New York, New York 10010, 1991).

to attach the butt section to the leader with a nail or needle knot. This is really a matter of personal preference.

There are three popular ways to connect the varying diameters of monofilament to build the sections in your tapered leader: a surgeon's knot, a conventional blood knot, or a simple blood knot. Certainly the surgeon's knot is the easiest and quickest to build, and in the larger diameters I still use it. But, what breaks in a leader is usually not the knot that ties the tippet to the fly, but the knot that attaches the tippet to the next larger strand of the leader. A surgeon's or blood knot will work here, but a knot that I developed through months of testing, the simple blood knot, is far superior, in my opinion.

When tied correctly, the simple blood knot will break only at full line-strength or within a few percentage points of it. I now use this knot whenever I am connecting monofilament strands of 12-pound test or smaller.

Generally, a saltwater tapered leader will be comprised of five sections: a butt section, three pieces for the mid-section, and a tippet of varying length, depending upon the angler's wishes. Adhering to that design, here is a basic formula for building saltwater tapered leaders that will serve you well: *make the butt section whatever length you desire, then make each strand of the mid-section one half the length of the section preceding it, followed by a 2-foot tippet.*

Following this formula, a typical leader for bonefish and permit is made up of a 5-foot butt section of 30-pound monofilament, followed by a 2 1/2-foot section of 25-pound monofilament, followed by an 18-inch section of 20-pound monofilament, followed by a 9-inch section of 15-pound monofilament, followed by a 2-foot tippet section of 10 or 12-pound monofilament. This design will give you a leader with a total length of nearly 12 feet. It is not necessary to have the various pieces exactly the lengths suggested, merely a decent approximation will do.

If you want to make the leader shorter or longer, simply decrease or increase the length of the butt section, and then follow the formula for halving the length of each new section of monofilament added.

Finally, keep this important point in mind: *using monofilament strands of the same apparent limpness will always produce a more efficient tapered leader.*

For most bonefish I prefer a leader tippet of 10-pound monofilament. This is supple enough to allow the small flies that are popularly used for bonefish to have their own movement on the retrieve. It is also stout enough to handle most bonefish. Or you can use 12-pound test in the new extra thin monofilament that is now being made available from several manufacturers, as its diameter is no larger than the older 10-pound material. But such thin monofilament sometimes doesn't have as good abrasion resistance as that of the older and larger monofilaments, so if you use it, I recommend you take great care to make the knot connection to the fly the very best you can.

My line testing machine says that the non-slip mono loop is nearly 100 percent in strength — so if you need a loop knot, this is my first choice. For just connecting a leader tippet to the hook, the Trilene knot, when properly tied, will almost always deliver 100 percent of line strength, which means in most cases the knot to the fly is as strong or stronger than the tippet. For permit fishing I use 12 or 15-pound-test tippets. I have not found either bonefish or permit to be particularly leader shy. I have experimented with tippets of varying strengths and diameters on both species, and have found that even using 20-pound leader tippets didn't discourage strikes if the fly had good action. But, since you are generally throwing heavier crab patterns to permit, a leader tippet of 15-

pound test is called for; it is more than supple enough to get the job done.

To repeat a caution made earlier in this text, don't use monofilament, especially tippets, that contrast too much with the bottom. For example, darkish brown tippets fished on a light sand bottom will often discourage bonefish from striking. Use clear or very lightly tinted tippets.

BONEFISH FLIES

Bonefish and permit flies require separate treatment, for only a few patterns are effective on permit, while just the reverse is true with bonefish.

Stomach analyses show that bonefish eat virtually anything they can get in their mouths — crabs, shrimp, worms, or just about anything else they can dig out from the bottom that looks worth eating. Scientists call this opportunistic feeding. So to better understand which fly patterns will work best on bonefish, we need briefly to consider their anatomy and how and where they feed.

The mouth of the bonefish is located near the base of its head, and the anatomy of the fish is such that it can successfully feed primarily on the bottom. Some anglers think bonefish feed only on the bottom. But I have caught many bonefish that took my flies in the middle of the water column. And I have even witnessed rare occasions when bonefish appeared to be sipping something from the surface. Anglers have told me they have caught bonefish on dry flies, and I *think* they may be telling the truth. My own experience tells me otherwise. After many years of casting scores of surface flies to hundreds of bonefish, I have never seen the least sign of interest from a bonefish. So I gave up on trying to catch them on surface flies a long time ago. I'm not saying it isn't possible. But heck, I like to catch bonefish, and I know using underwater flies is a far more productive pathway to success.

Bonefish are found on different types of flats' bottom. Some flats' bottoms are carpeted with thick turtle grass, some with totally white sand — or a mixture of sand and what looks to me like an alga — while some are completely littered with leader-cutting fragmented coral. Of course, water depth on the flats varies considerably with tidal action, but we usually fly fish for bonefish on very shallow flats, rarely in more than four feet of water. I would guess that perhaps more than half of all bonefish are caught in water less than two feet deep. But generally, large bonefish, those exceeding nine pounds, will not be found in shallow water. I can think of only a few exceptions to this, such as Shell Key at Islamorada, Florida. But the general rule is that bigger fish will be closer to deep water (a channel or hole), as they prefer to feed in water that at least covers their backs.

Bonefish have a very small mouth. The small mouth of even a 10-pounder will surprise someone the first time he's lucky enough to land and examine one. So the first prerequisite for selecting a bonefish fly is size. Patterns dressed on large hooks are going to be nearly worthless.

Many years ago, anglers thought that bonefish didn't readily take flies at all. One of the principal reasons they had reached this conclusion, I think, was that fishermen were casting patterns dressed on big #1/0 to #3/0 hooks. Joe Brooks, who really got the fly-fishing public interested in fishing for bonefish, used flies in sizes ranging from #1/0 to #3/0 when he first pursued the species seriously. As a consequence, for some years after Joe caught and wrote about the first bonefish he took on a fly, large hooks were the standard.

Bart Foth, a Pennsylvania angler who vacationed each winter in the Keys, annually won the MET Tournament (the largest fishing tournament of that time, located in South Florida). Every year Bart would catch the biggest bonefish, and he held the tournament record for years.

At that time, I was manager of the tournament, and it was one of my duties to examine the leader and fly that caught any record fish. Foth came to me and said he would enter a tourney record and give me the leader for examination — but only if I would not divulge the fly he was using. I agreed and was stunned when I found that it was tied on a *relatively small #4 hook*, dressed with a thin yellow chenille body and a short wisp of white bucktail.

I kept that secret for a long time, although I did get Bart to allow me to fish the same fly. My number of catches rose incredibly when I started using such smaller flies.

I'm certain that Bart Foth was the first person that used very small flies for bonefish. Joe Brooks made people realize that catching bonefish on a fly was practical, and Bart Foth made the next innovation when he developed the correct size for the bonefish fly pattern.

If I were required to fly fish for bonefish with only one hook size, then a #4 hook with a regular shank length would be my first choice. Among experienced bonefishermen, the largest hook size I ever see being used now is a #1/0, the smallest a #8.

If the water is low on the flats, then a #6 or no bigger than a #4 should be used. On very shallow flats with small bonefish, a #8 often works well.

I once even tried fishing patterns with #10 hooks. I recall it was late in the afternoon, on very calm water. Large bonefish were working right at the top of the water column, either tailing or swimming with their backs protruding out of the water. They were as spooky as a cat in a dog pound. At the slightest hint of danger they were gone, and even a #6 fly dropping to the surface would spook them. So I dressed some #10 hooks with a pattern that consisted mainly of simply a wing and a little body, so that the fly could sort of parachute to the water with almost no splash. The fish often ignored these flies (maybe because they were so small), and even when I did get a hook-up and the fish took off, I usually lost it. I think the reason that I lost the fish was because a #10 hook has such a small bite area that little of the fish's mouth was being impaled on the hook, and it was able to tear free easily.

To only a slightly lesser degree, I think a similar problem exists in using a #8 hook: it's okay on small bonefish, I suppose, and while an occasional large fish may be landed on a #8 hook, the chances of grass and debris accumulating on the line when a bonefish makes a long run are so common that frequently such a small hook will pull loose from the fish.

After more than 30 years of fishing for bonefish in many areas of the world, I am convinced, however, that *big* bonefish do want larger flies. After all, while an elephant will eat peanuts, it doesn't make its living on them. Big bonefish like big flies. They will most definitely take flies much larger than those consumed by smaller fish. I call a big fly one that is dressed on a #4 hook or larger. My favorite hook size for large bonefish is a #2. If you are seeking bonefish that top eight pounds, a #2 hook is not too large and even specially tied patterns on hooks as large as a #1 or #1/0 are not out of place, so long as they can be presented so that they don't impact too heavily when they contact the surface. This splash can be minimized by the method used in dressing the fly. Obviously, one with lead eyes and a sleek body will hit the water with more noise than one that is tied with a fluffy wing of deer hair.

Generally, bonefish flies that match the color of the bottom will be the best choice. This is because bonefish have been feeding on saltwater flats for eons. And to help camouflage themselves from bonefish predators and aid in their survival, bonefish prey species have evolved over time into colors resembling that of the bottoms upon which they live.

The only exception I have found to this is at Christmas Island in the Pacific. Somehow, on the incredibly white sand flats at Christmas Island, the black crab with a red claw has bucked Darwinism and remained highly visible to bonefish. So, a small bonefish fly tied with a black chenille body and a tuft of red calf tail successfully tricks the bonefish there.

But, this is the only exception that comes to my mind. In all cases, using bonefish flies that compare favorably with the bottom coloration will produce more fish over the long run. For example, if you are fishing the predominately white flats of the Bahamas, then white, light tan, and pale pink seem to be the best colors. On the other hand, if you fish in the Keys, where the flats are often carpeted in brownish-olive turtle grass, then brown or tan flies seem to outfish those that are lighter in color.

Pete Perinchief, famed angler of Bermuda, was responsible for the next breakthrough in bonefish fly pattern design. Pete is one of the best light tackle fishermen I have ever known, with a mind that is constantly working. Realizing that the best way to retrieve a fly is right on the bottom, since that is where most bonefish take their food, Pete designed a fly with the wing tied in a manner that was just the reverse of standard fly patterns. His pattern was designed with an inverted wing that caused the hook point to ride upright. This accomplished two desirable things. First, the hook snagged far less frequently on the

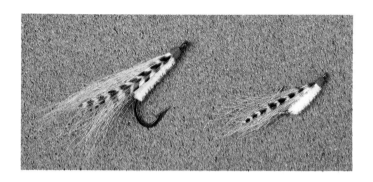

Styles of Bonefish Flies: At left is shown the old style, tied on a #1/0 hook; at right is the size now being used most often, tied on a #4 hook.

bottom. And second, just as importantly, the hook point was riding up, poised in a better position to hook a bonefish that grabbed the fly.

Pete named this new pattern the Horror (in honor of his daughter) and today, it is still one of the finest patterns for bonefish. In slightly deeper water, but less than a foot deep, especially on a grass-covered bottom, a Horror-type pattern is ideal.

The next major innovation in fly patterns was developed by Bob Nauheim, of Santa Rosa, California, when he developed his famous Crazy Charlie pattern. Actually, Bob named it the Nasty Charlie, but a well-known fly-fishing company renamed it the Crazy Charlie and that name stuck with the public.

Like Perinchief's Horror, the fly is tied so that it rides with the hook point up. What makes the Crazy Charlie really different is that it is sparsely dressed and carries either bead-chain or lead eyes at the front of the hook. This causes the fly to dive quickly to the bottom. Before Bob developed this concept, sinking bonefish flies had lead wrapped on the hook shank, which was then covered by some material. They sank, but not rapidly.

The most recent innovation in bonefish flies has been to construct them with epoxy or hot glue. These patterns, which can be shaped to resemble small crabs, shrimp, or the other creatures bonefish feed upon, have their own unique action in the water. They work well in open water and in grassy areas, provided they have been constructed with stiff monofilament weedguards.

When bonefish are feeding on flats carpeted in grass, in calm water so shallow that a portion of their backs protrudes above the surface — as they frequently do — they are usually quite nervous. Throwing a lead-eyed Crazy Charlie or a wide-bodied epoxy fly near such spooky fish is going to spell trouble for the angler. The splashdown of these type patterns is too much. What is needed instead for this type presentation is a fly that comes to the calm surface like a feather; one, moreover, that will work well in the grass without fouling. The best patterns for these bonefishing situations are those tied in a fashion similar

Bendback Fly Patterns. The fly shown at left is tied incorrectly: too much wing is separated from the body. At right is a Bendback pattern tied correctly.

to the Horror, or a Bendback pattern, as shown on the previous page. This pattern is very effective where debris and grass exist, and the retrieve must be made through it.

Nor are Crazy Charlie flies recommended when fishing on a flats' bottom that contains debris, coral, or heavy turtle grass, as the pattern's protruding eyes will frequently become entangled in such obstructions. A Crazy Charlie tied with the eyes omitted (called a Blind Charlie) will frequently do better in this situation.

But where the bottom is relatively free of impediments, the Crazy Charlie really comes into its own as a super bonefish fly. The fly can be dropped to the clean bottom and hopped along on a fast retrieve. When the retrieve is stopped, the fly drops back down to the bottom like a miniature jig — a motion that bonefish can go crazy over!

One of the characteristics that I really like about the Crazy Charlie patterns is that they are tied rather sleekly, with weighted eyes, so that — assuming you can develop high line speed — when you are casting into the wind they will turn over quite well; whereas flies that are tied in a more fluffy pattern will be blown back at the end of the cast, spoiling the presentation.

Another superb bonefish fly I would like to bring to your attention is the Clouser Deep Minnow, which was developed by Bob Clouser, of Middletown, Pennsylvania. Bob developed this pattern for freshwater fishing. It has since become one of the most effective underwater flies in fresh or saltwater. For quick-diving presentations when working over a clear bottom, this pattern has replaced the Crazy Charlie as my favorite bonefish fly.

The Clouser Deep Minnow is a very simple fly to tie. Place a #2 hook in the vise. Attach about 3/16 inch behind the hook eye a pair of lead eyes of size 1/50 ounce (5/32 inch). If I have to fish in deep water I will use lead eyes size 1/36 (3/16 inch). Turn the hook over in the vise so that the hook points up. Just in front of the eyes, tie in some white bucktail (about the same diameter as an old wooden barn burner match). The white bucktail wing should be about 2 3/4 inches long. On top of the white wing secure about eight strands of pearl-colored Crystal Flash of the same length. On top of that tie in chartreuse bucktail of the same amount as used in the white wing. Then cement the head, and that's it! You can also tie the Clouser Deep Minnow pattern in an alternate tan coloration that on some flats' bottoms is very effective, simply by replacing the chartreuse bucktail wing with a wing the color of khaki.

I always fish the Clouser Deep Minnow in one or the other of these two color patterns. However, my first and most effective choice is the chartreuse pattern. But if several fish turn it down, I will switch colors. Only if I have gotten several refusals of both color patterns from big fish (which rarely happens if the presentation is good) will I then switch to another fly.

My most successful day on big bonefish came on the west side of Andros Island in the Bahamas one summer day, when I and a friend, Irv Swope, together caught 36 bonefish weighing more than six pounds. Four of them weighed more than 10 pounds, and one topped 11 pounds! All of them were caught on a Clouser Deep Minnow in either the chartreuse or khaki color.

The Clouser casts like a dream — almost as easy as a conventional bonefish fly — and its contact with the surface is soft. It sinks rapidly to the bottom, with the hook riding up.

Finally, deciding which bonefish fly to use is often best answered by asking your guide. Bonefish guides fish their local flats daily and know what patterns have been effec-

Typical fast-sinking bonefish flies. From left to right, top row: Crazy Charlie, black/red; Crazy Charlie; Gotcha (formerly McVay Charlie); Crazy Charlie, brown; middle row: Crazy Charlie, orange (formerly Gotcha); Clouser Deep Minnow, white/chartreuse; Clouser Deep Minnow, white/tan; Woodstock White; bottom row: four examples of epoxy and hot-glue flies.

tive most recently (or just as importantly, what patterns are not currently working). For example, once when I asked Rupert Leadon, who runs the Andros Island Bonefish Club in the Bahamas, what fly to use, I couldn't believe his response! He handed me a brilliant orange pattern, which he called a "Gotcha." The original Gotcha, conceived by Jim McVay, Sr., was an orange pattern (the Gotcha most anglers refer to today is a white Crazy Charlie with a long pink nose). But this orange fly seemed ridiculous. Yet even so, since I have made it a rule over the years to always follow the suggestions of a good guide, I tied it on. And what do you think happened? The fish

Typical bonefish fly patterns for use in medium-depth water.
From left to right, top row: *Lefty's, pink/yellow; Lefty's, green/brown; Bad Day Fly;* bottom row: *Agent Orange; Snapping Shrimp; Bonefish Special; Monteague's Minnow.*

Typical bonefish fly patterns for use in shallow water or for use on flats with grass bottom. From left to right, top row: *Mitey Mite; Sand's Bonefish Fly; two examples of a Mini Puff;* bottom row: *Horror; two examples of a Pfleuger's Hair Shrimp; Don's Special.*

seemed to fall all over themselves to get at that fly! But, I can tell you, after many other wasted hours of casting, there are places and days on these same Bahamian flats where and when a bright orange fly produced the same result as throwing a grenade in the water.

PERMIT FLIES

Permit, along with mutton snapper, are perhaps the two most difficult fish to catch on the fly in shallow-water flats. The permit is so easily spooked that for many years we felt that perhaps the fish simply couldn't be taken well on flies. We now know that's not so.

Anglers have known for many years that one of the best live baits for permit is a crab the size of a U.S. quarter or half dollar. Now fly patterns resembling a crab of that size have been developed that will really get the job done on the wily permit. (Incidentally, I have tried many crab imitations in such small sizes on bonefish, because I know bonefish eat crabs. I've seen them do it. But after many attempts at presenting crab patterns of many designs to bonefish, I feel that other bonefish flies are much better strike producers. So, I no longer use crab patterns of any kind or size in fly fishing for bonefish.)

Several types of crab patterns have been developed. Most of them are made either of epoxy, or a combination of epoxy and deer hair, or some weighted paste material that hardens after it is applied to the body. The principal drawback of crab patterns dressed with deer hair is that deer hair will resist sinking rapidly. To offset this, some tyers position heavy epoxy or other hard material on the bottom of the fly. But it is much better to construct the pattern from something other than deer hair, some substance that will sink quicker and thus not require heavy application of epoxy or other hard material.

A poor design factor in many crab patterns is that the entire bottom surface is coated in epoxy or a hard material. When such a fly strikes the flat surface it is similar to slamming a ping-pong paddle down on a flat table. It makes too much noise.

Furthermore, the requirement of having to throw a heavily weighted fly to a precise target, and if it gets there, having it land on the water without too much impact, is a major problem for many casters — especially those who are new to saltwater fly fishing. Epoxy and other patterns with a lot of hard material on the belly of the pattern simply complicate and increase the caster's difficulties.

A well-designed crab pattern should have the following characteristics: it should imitate a crab shape; it should cast easily; it should contact the surface softly; and it should imitate the swimming characteristics of the crab.

Del Brown's Permit Flies

Fortunately, such a pattern has been developed, and in my view — as well as that of many other saltwater fly fishermen, professionals and amateurs alike — it is vastly superior to all other existing crab patterns, at least at this writing. The pattern is Del Brown's Permit Fly, which is also popularly called "Del's Merkin." It was developed by Californian Del Brown, a widely experienced saltwater angler who to date has caught more than one hundred permit on a fly and holds two IGFA world records — one for a 41 1/2-pounder caught on an *8-pound-test tippet* on a flat near Key West (the largest permit ever taken on a fly rod); and the other for a 9 3/4-pound permit caught on 2-pound-test tippet. During the first two years of use, this fly was responsible for catching more than 200 permit.

Del Brown's Permit Fly is easy to tie (as shown on the opposite page). Here's how: (Step 1) Attach 1/24-ounce lead eyes at the head of the hook near the eye, and tie in several one-inch cree feathers along with two or three strands of bright-colored Flashabou that are splayed at the back, like frog legs. Del uses chartreuse tying thread, as he believes this makes the fly more alluring to permit. (Step 2A and 2B) Then at a 90-degree angle to the hook, tie a series of two-inch lengths of khaki and dark-brown rug yarn. (Step 3) Trim to a crab shape and separate the yarn. (Step 4) Tie in about four short lengths of rubber bands. (Step 5) Trim the bands so that they extend about a 1/2 inch beyond the body to resemble the legs on a crab. And finally, tint the tips of the rubber bands red with a permanent marking pen. The finished pattern has a crab-shaped body approximately 1 inch long and 3/4 inch wide, or about the size of a U.S. quarter.

Most of the time, Del uses 1/24-ounce lead eyes on the pattern. But in situations where the bottom is very shallow and the water slick and calm, so that eyes of this

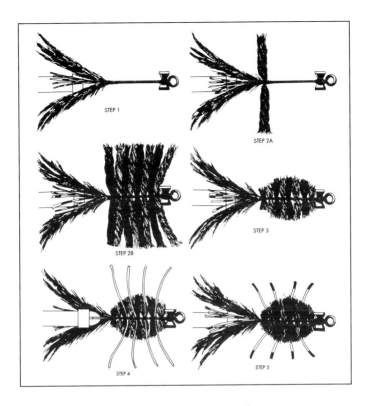

STEP 1

STEP 2A

STEP 2B

STEP 3

STEP 4

STEP 5

Tying Instructions for Del Brown's Permit Fly

weight would create too much splash, he switches to patterns tied with lighter 1/36-ounce lead eyes. And for those rare occasions when he wants to get the fly to dive deeper, he uses patterns tied with 1/18-ounce lead eyes.

He uses rug yarn of khaki and dark brown for about 90 percent of his flies. But, when he is fishing on flats that are light in color and are probably harboring the white ghost crab — a favorite food of permit — he switches to a yarn color of either all dark cream or all light tan.

Here are the reasons why Del Brown's Permit Fly has

become the most popular and effective fly pattern among knowledgeable permit fishermen. Only lead eyes weighing no more than 1/24 ounce are used. They are enough when combined with the rug yarn to sink the fly. And most importantly, because lead eyes are located at one end of the fly, the pattern tilts to the side and dives at a steep angle toward the bottom. This exactly imitates live crab behavior . . . this is precisely what a crab does when it sees a permit or other predator. The soft rug yarn material produces a much softer impact than patterns that employ

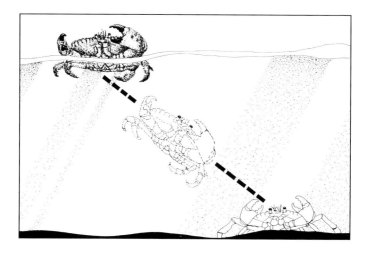

ABOVE: *Typical Descent of Crab.* RIGHT: *Del Brown's Permit Fly Descending to Bottom at Steep Angle*

The Clouser Deep Minnow. Top fly is dressed for bonefish, with lighter 1/50-ounce lead eyes; bottom fly is dressed for permit, with a slightly heavier wing and heavier 1/24-ounce lead eyes.

a hard coating on the belly of the fly. And most importantly, it is a pattern that is easy to cast.

The Clouser Deep Minnow, described earlier in the section on bonefish flies, has lately begun to be used on permit. To date, according to reports I have received, it has already accounted for more than 50 permit hook-ups. The Clouser pattern, in the adaptation being used for permit, is tied on a #1 hook, with 1/24-ounce lead eyes, and a wing of a specific color. The underwing is tied with white bucktail, on top of which are placed a half-dozen strands of pearl-colored Crystal Flash. On top of that is secured some chartreuse-colored bucktail. This is a very sleek fly, with a wing of 2 1/2 to no more than 3 inches.

Overleaf: *Christmas Island punts heading out for a day of bonefishing.*

CHAPTER THREE

TECHNIQUES FOR BONEFISH

WADING

When you reach a wading flat, strip off less line than you would when working from a boat. When wading, you can't usually see as far as you can from the elevated position in a boat, so longer casts are generally not required. And though I frequently catch bonefish beyond 60 feet — whether from a boat or wading — in the wading mode I rarely pull more than 40 feet of line and leader, combined, from the reel, because I'm going to have to transport this amount of line outside the rod tip as I wade. The more line you carry outside the rod tip, the more likely you are to foul the leader, or the line, or both.

There are several ways you can carry line while wading. None of them is perfect and all will eventually cause you problems. One of the best ways — to give a right-handed example, that is, assuming you are casting with your right hand — is to hold the fly in the first finger and thumb of your left hand, but with the hook pointing away from you. This will prevent the hook from catching you or your clothing when you cast. Loop the mid-portion of the leader across one of the other fingers of your left hand.

This procedure permits you to carry all of the leader under control. Form several large loops of the fly line outside the rod tip and drape them over the little finger of the right hand gripping the rod. Using this technique you can carry a 14-foot leader and about 30 feet of line as you wade, and rarely experience any problems.

When the flats' bottom is fairly clean, there is another way to carry line outside the fly rod tip-top. I use this method often. Pull off about 20 feet of fly line. Combined with the leader, you will then have outside the rod tip a total of about 30 feet of line and leader. As you slowly wade, simply roll cast the fly ahead of you. When you have moved forward a number of steps, make another roll cast. This works extremely well when the wind is behind you, as it will assist you in making the roll cast. Walk forward only far enough so that you can make an easy roll cast. Roll cast at a 45-degree angle above the horizon to

Method of Holding Line While Wading

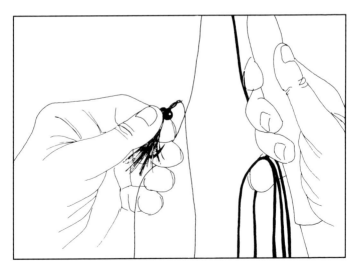

*Orvis
Shooting
Basket*

assist in picking up the fly and laying it out in front of you again. This puts most of the line in front of you while you are wading, and you are always ready to make a quick back cast and presentation if a fish is spotted.

Or, you may want to consider using a shooting basket. Bluefish anglers from New England have devised an ingenious shooting basket that you can use on the flats. You can construct one quite easily.*

Also, Orvis recently began offering a commercial version of a shooting basket. I've tested it on bonefish flats, and it works very well. I highly recommend it.

To use a shooting basket, make the longest cast you will need and carefully retrieve the line back into the basket. Now you can wade and search for fish. It's amazing how well you can shoot line from it. I don't ever attempt to strip the fly line back into the basket while making the retrieve. Instead, I allow my retrieved line to drop on the surface of the water. When I begin to look for a new fish,

---

*Note: See a companion volume in the Library, *Lefty's Little Tips*, pages 139-140.

I again strip the line back carefully into the basket. Of course, a shooting basket can also be used on a boat deck. It's quite handy there too, particularly if there is an incredibly strong wind blowing.

FISHING FROM A BOAT DECK

Of all the things that plague a fly fishermen working from the front deck of a flats' boat, getting the line tangled as he makes a cast to a fish is one of the most vexing. We spend hours or even days tying flies, getting our tackle ready, and traveling to our destination. Then, after some searching, we see the fish and make the necessary cast — only to have the line tangle and ruin our presentation.

Although line-tangling will to some degree always be with us, particularly in the windy conditions that exist on the saltwater flats, there are many things you can do to lessen this problem.

When you first step up on the casting platform of a flats' boat and pull off line, you must take one precaution. The line being pulled from the reel is falling to the casting deck on top of the line underneath it. If you then cast with the line in this position, a tangled mess may occur. This is because the forward portion of your fly line is lying on the bottom of the pile of line you pulled from the reel. To eliminate this problem, simply pull off line, make a false cast over the water, and then when you strip the line back in, it will be lying in the proper position.

When working from a boat, another mistake made even by some experienced fly fishermen is that they pull more line off the reel than they need. The more loose line on the deck, the more you increase your chances of a foul-up. So only strip the amount of line from the reel needed to get your fly to the target. For most bonefish, permit, (and tarpon) situations, if you are a pretty good caster, a maximum of 50 feet of line stripped off the reel is all the line you will need for 90 to 95 percent of the casting opportunities you will have. Del Brown makes a foot-long mark on his fly line at 50 feet with a permanent marking pen. He strips off line until he sees this long mark, makes his cast, retrieves the line, and he's ready.

Even when you have taken these precautions, on windy days your line will have a tendency to blow all over the place. A piece of netting placed over the deck area below your feet may help, but a bucket or container is also

Typical Line-Holding Container

helpful. One of the best containers is one of those plastic boxes that milk cartons are transported in. They are light, sit well on the deck in a breeze, and are fairly stable, since the wind blows freely through the holes in the woven pattern of the box. Make the longest cast you think you'll need. Then strip the line in and allow it to fall inside the container. When you see a fish, make the cast and the line will flow out of the bucket and almost never tangle.

One problem you will frequently confront when standing on the deck of a flats' boat in a "ready to fish" position on a windy day is that the line that hangs down from the reel spool, along with the loop of line you are holding in your hand, often become tangled together by the breeze. To avoid this, I now use a neat trick shown to me by Captain Flip Pallot, of Homestead, Florida, one of the leading Florida Keys guides. As shown in the illustration below, about 18 inches from where your line exits the reel spool, tuck it in your belt in a "U" shape. Just push a loop of it behind the belt. This keeps this line and the loop hanging in the hand from tangling with one another.

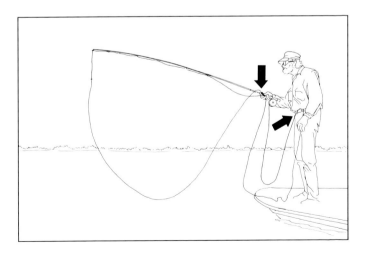

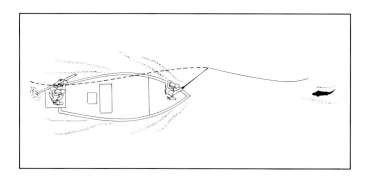

Incorrect Boat Casting Position

When a cast is made, the speed of the cast is more than enough to drag out the line looped under your belt, and it will not spoil your cast. Neat trick!

When being poled in a boat for any kind of flats fishing, the caster must always be aware of the person doing the poling. Safety is important. *Never make a cast directly ahead, or you will likely hook the person poling behind you. Allow the poler to turn the boat to one side so that you can make a clear, safe back cast.*

Correct Boat Casting Position

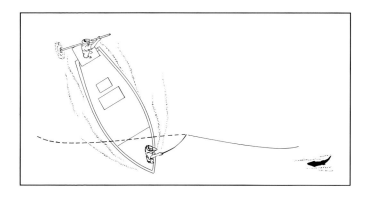

Locating bonefish is quite similar to squirrel hunting. A hunter doesn't look for a sleek animal with a long, fluffy tail. Instead, he searches for a small rounded lump, a wisp of hair that moves on the breeze as the tail is blown, or other indicators that really look nothing like the animal at all. Many a tree knot has been blasted by hunters who figured it was the head of a squirrel.

Bonefish are often extremely difficult to see, because like tarpon and permit, their silvery sides act like a mirror, reflecting the environment over which they move. You seldom really see a full-shaped fish, just as you hardly ever see the full-figure of a squirrel.

But, there are other indicators that often help you locate bonefish — even at considerable distance. For example, while many anglers don't realize it, bonefish feed avidly on small minnows and baitfish. If you are on a flat where you suspect bonefish are cruising, and you see a vague spray of small silvery baitfish — you should assume there is an excellent chance they are spooking from one or more bonefish.

While there will be some exceptions, when feeding on a flat most bonefish will approach it from a fairly specific direction and proceed across the flat in that same general direction. So always try to quickly ascertain the swimming direction of the fish, and then you can plan how best to approach them.

One of the first things you learn about seeing any fish on the flats is that you have to adjust your way of looking for it according to the water depth. *If the fish is in water less than a foot deep, you should look at the surface*. A fish as large as a bonefish will create a surface wake — or "V" shape — as it moves through shallow water. On a calm surface such a "V" shape can often be seen as far away as 100 yards. If glare or other light conditions permit you to observe the "V"-shaped wake, but you can't actually see the fish, remember that the wake will be behind the fish. If you want to make a cast in this situation, direct your fly five or six feet in front of the wake.

When the water is more than a foot deep, most of the time you will not see a wake. You may see what is termed "nervous water" — a rippling of the surface that is unlike any other ripple in the immediate area. This is especially evident with a school of cruising bonefish. The faster the school moves, the more agitated the water appears. Also, if you observe small waves rolling across a flat, but also see a wave that is moving in a direction different from the regular wave pattern, you should assume that it's probably being created by bonefish.

In water more than one foot deep, *the trick for seeing fish is not to look at the surface, but at the bottom*. When searching for bonefish in one to four feet of water, the mistake many anglers make is to look at the surface. So you can understand why you need to look at the bottom in this tactical situation, let me give you an analogy.

If you are standing on one side of a street, looking at cars that are driving by immediately in front of you, all you will see is those cars. If two people were strolling on the far pavement across the street from you, even though they were in your same line of sight, you would probably not notice them. But, if you instead focused your attention on the two people, when a car passed between you and them, you would see the car, as it would interrupt your vision and then capture your attention. In similar fashion, if you look intently at the bottom of a flat in several feet of water, anything that moves through the water column between you and the bottom can be detected. That is a

Sometimes a bonefish's shadow is easier to see than the fish.

major key to seeing bonefish in two to three feet of water.

But I will caution you that bonefish that are moving sideways or at right angles to you are very hard to see, especially if you are wading. You are looking at the side of the fish, and its side, again acting like a mirror, reflects back the bottom over which the fish is swimming.

The easiest bonefish to see are those that are coming directly at or away from you. Because in these situations, you are in a position to see the darker back of the fish which is not giving off a mirror effect.

And, of course, the higher you are above the surface, the easier all bonefish are to see.

There is one characteristic of flats' fish that will always assist you in locating them. Because of tidal action, usually most of the fish working a flat will move in the same general direction. There may be the odd fish that will not follow this pattern. But be aware that when the first few bonefish, permit (or tarpon), that come to view appear to be coming from a specific direction, it's probable that for some time during that particular tidal stage almost all other fish will be traveling along that same path.

Mud is also an excellent tip-off for locating bonefish.

When there are exceptionally low spring tides, for example, in many areas of the world the flats go entirely dry and the bonefish have to find somewhere else to feed. Often a huge school will concentrate in a deep basin, tearing up the bottom to find food. This creates a huge, muddy area that is clearly distinguished from the clear water surrounding it. I've seen such muds that were a mile long and a half mile wide — or even larger. Cruise the outside of the muddy water and try to locate the brightest mud; that's the source where the bonefish will be feeding. Tie on a fast-sinking fly, like a Clouser Deep Minnow, Crazy Charlie, or any fly that sinks well. Cast out, allow the fly to get to the bottom, and make short six-inch line strips. If you have located the school of bonefish, strikes will soon be forthcoming.

In such a mud you can land many bonefish, and usually the one you are fighting doesn't seem to alarm the others. I don't find this kind of bonefish particularly interesting. It's too easy. But it is certainly an effective method of catching them. And hey! It's fly fishing! It beats working!

Another kind of mud that will tip you off to the presence of bonefish may come into view as your boat is being poled along a mangrove island. If you see a small patch of mud, say several feet in diameter, close by the mangrove roots, the chances that a bonefish is working the area are excellent. So be on the lookout.

Another mud condition that has helped anglers catch many bonefish is the single puff. This occurs when a bonefish tilts its head and either worries something out of the bottom or jets a stream of water from its mouth to blast the creature from the bottom. In either case a small puff of mud, roughly a foot in diameter, is created in the water. If you see one of these muds that is fading and becoming almost indistinct, look around. Chances are there's a bonefish nearby. You may be able to spot a more distinct puff of mud closer by where the bonefish has moved and is currently feeding.

CASTING

The first objective of casting the fly to a fish is to deliver it within the fish's feeding range in a manner that doesn't alert or alarm the fish. Yet, on the saltwater flats I continually see anglers making an overhead cast to bonefish. They bring their rod forward in a vertical — or near-vertical — position and shoot their fly to the target. I consider the overhead cast a major reason why anglers frighten flats' species. It is extremely poor flats' fly-fishing technique, producing two bad results. First, the unrolling line comes toward the fish high and overhead, making it quite possible for the fish to see the approaching line, especially in bright sunlight that may produce rod or line reflection. Secondly, since as an overhead cast unrolls, it tends to sweep the fly over much as a vertical crack-the-whip motion does; if there is excessive energy placed in the cast (which often happens in an adrenaline-charged bonefishing situation) the fly will be thrown over and down to the surface with a hard impact. Either of these factors can obviously spoil a presentation and frighten the fish.

Never make an overhead cast to fish that may be easily spooked, unless you have no choice. And if an overhead cast must be made, care should be taken to deliver it with only enough energy to carry the fly to the target.

There are four much better flats' casts that I try to use whenever I can. First is simply a side cast. This keeps the line low to the water so the fish are not liable to see it, and produces a quieter presentation. It is my standard flats' cast.

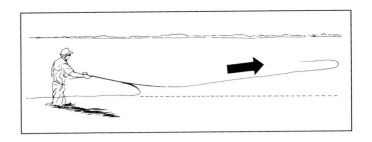

The Side Cast

A second useful flats' cast is a slow, low, climbing cast. The rod is brought forward at about a 45-degree angle from the water, with the fly aimed at an angle slightly above the head. The fly will go in the direction that the rod speeds up and stops at the end of the cast. The moment this speed-up-and-stop occurs, I drop the rod tip to the surface. This move drags the line down to the surface and slows it down, and because the fly is aimed slightly above the surface, as it descends it also assists in dragging on the line as it is unrolling, helping to bring the fly to the surface very, very softly.

I frequently use a variation of this same cast when the wind is blowing from the side, since accuracy suffers when you make an overhead cast directly at the fish and sideways to the wind — the wind blows the fly to one side and the fly usually falls well to the downwind side of the target. In such a situation, aim the fly just above head level (you can use either an overhead or a side cast — but I prefer the side cast) and the moment the tip stops its forward motion, drop the tip underwater. This will drag the line into the water and prevent it from being blown off course. But since the fly will go in the direction that the rod tip speeds up and stops, this procedure will not alter the fly's direction.

Another great cast that I use frequently, especially when wading and there is a wind at my back, is the roll cast. With it, you can pick a fly up and roll it forward so gently that when the fly hits the water, you can barely see the little blip. It makes for a very delicate presentation, especially with small #4 and #6 flies.

There are two schools of thought on casting flies to flats' fish. One suggests making long casts; the other recommends that you wait until the fish is very close, usually as close as 40 feet or even closer.

The first school (to which I subscribe) believes that *if you can cast accurately with confidence*, making a long cast has a great advantage over a shorter presentation. Bonefish (and permit) frequently change course, or perhaps simply don't see your fly on the first presentation. And obviously, the farther away the fish is, the less likely it is to be aware of you. A long cast will let you offer the fly to the fish a first time, and if that cast fails, allow you the time to make another cast to the same fish.

The short-range school believes that people tend to spook fish at long ranges because their accuracy suffers at such distances. They believe that it is much better to wait until everything is just right so that a more accurate short cast can be made.

But I would guess that more than half of all the bonefish I have caught are hooked at distances exceeding 45 feet. For example, recently while fishing the flats at Los Roques with guide, Alex Gonzalez, I caught three fish by casting the full fly line. Once I even used six feet of my backing! These were fish that were crossing at a distance. Alex and I determined they would never likely come closer, so we decided to take a shot at them.

If you can handle your line well at a distance, I see no reason whatsoever why you shouldn't fish that way.

A number of Florida Keys bonefish guides disagree with me on this issue. They tell me that since few of their clients can spot bonefish at ranges greater than 50 feet or so, there is little need for them to encourage long blind casts. I agree with that, of course. But there are many times on the flats — particularly on clear white sand bottoms — when fish can easily be spotted at quite a long range. And if one has the ability to make an accurate cast at long distance — and I emphasize again, *if one has the ability to make an accurate long cast with confidence* — I see no harm in this technique.

PRESENTING THE FLY, RETRIEVING, AND STRIKING FISH

One of the major reasons that most fly fishermen fail is that they do not realize the importance of how the fly should approach the fish.

Let me cite just one example: I fished with an experienced freshwater angler last year at Christmas Island. This is perhaps the best place in the world — at least of all the places where I have fished for bonefish — to learn how to catch them. There are days at Christmas Island when anglers will see well over *1,000 bonefish* — usually in singles, doubles, or small schools. Christmas Island also has some of the best wading flats anywhere.

Inching our way across one of these flats, my friend and I saw three bonefish approaching, swimming very close together. They were going to pass slightly to our right as they headed for a nearby channel. When they were about 35 feet away, my companion made a cast that dropped the fly four feet beyond and six feet in front of the fish. He started to retrieve, and suddenly all three bonefish flushed wildly and tore off quickly into the safety of the channel.

What happened was typical of what I see occurring so many times. Like my friend, many anglers will deliver their cast so quietly that the fish will not spook. Their fly will drop exactly where they wanted it to. And apparently the fish will not have seen the anglers, either. But no hook-up! And even after repeated failures of this sort, few anglers seem to know what went wrong.

A basic principle of retrieve had been violated by my friend and these other anglers. Their presentation brought the fly a reasonable distance from the fish, but as the retrieve brought the fly closer, the fish had already moved so far forward that the fly was now actually being retrieved from an angle behind the bonefish. This was an unnatural approach for a prey species to be making toward a predator, and so the fish instinctively fled.

No fly should ever be retrieved so that the predator may think it is being attacked. Predators chase and eat their prey. Never in the natural environment does a crab pick a fight with a permit nor does a baitfish chase a barracuda. Predators have learned to expect to see their prey (or its imitation, the fly) act and react in the natural manner of any frightened creature that might be in danger. And when any other behavior is exhibited by the prey, the reaction of the predator is simply to back off or just leave.

Whenever we present a fly to a fish, the fly must be retrieved so that it behaves as all other prey that the fish consumes. *This principle, that a fly must be presented and retrieved in a natural manner, is more important, by far, than the type of fly, its color, size, or sink rate.*

Let's take a look at a typical example. The angler — whether wading or standing on the deck of a flats' boat — sees a fish ahead of him. Since a basic tenet of good fly presentation is never to throw the line over a fish, what many fishermen do is make a cast so that only the leader falls to the surface in front of the fish. The fly is then brought back in hopes the fish will strike it. But, from the fish's viewpoint, it sees the fly swimming toward it!

So what should you do in such a situation? Instead of presenting the fly so that it lands beyond the fish, cast it so that it falls to the water several feet to one side and a slight distance forward of the fish. Then begin your retrieve. What the fish now apparently sees is a creature that is sneaking off to the side, and it will frequently react to this movement by bolting forward and grabbing your fly.

Or, you may be faced with a situation where a fish is lying in a channel, and shrimp, crabs, and other morsels are being brought toward it, drifting with the tide. It would be unnatural for the fish to see these creatures swimming upcurrent against the tide — that's not normal

Incorrect Presentation and Retrieve — the fly is swimming towards the fish.

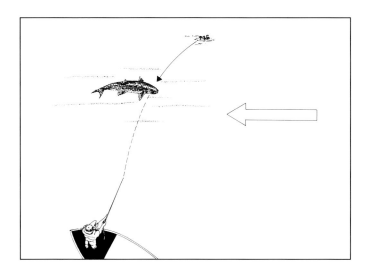

prey behavior. In this type situation, your cast should be made so that the fly will sweep down to one side of the fish, and just before it reaches the fish, make a "U-turn." This is what occurs frequently in the current. Downstream, a prey creature suddenly sees something that might eat it, so it tries to go sideways, rather than continue to drift toward the fish. *A fly that appears to sweep down on the current directly in front of the fish, and then makes a turn away, is the most natural of all retrieves.*

Second only to spooking fish with a bad cast, I find *incorrect fly presentation and retrieving technique to be the principal reason why anglers fail to score well on flats' fish.*

My favorite presentation and retrieving technique on an approaching bonefish, especially if it is a wise old single, is to pick out a spot on the flat between me and the approaching fish — it could be a dark hunk of coral, a tuft of grass, anything that is noticeable — and make a cast to that spot. When the fish approaches to within a foot of my fly, I start my retrieve. This method allows me to make casts that will not spook fish, even with heavy flies.

And while it seems silly to mention it, one of the most important factors in presenting the fly is to *always be aware of where the fly landed.* If it appears for sure that the fish is not going to see your fly, make another cast, keeping in mind that since a silent pick-up for a back cast is vital to not spooking the fish, you should lift all of the line off the water before making the back cast.

There are a variety of other tactical situations you will encounter on the flats. One is the tailing fish, a fish that is positioned vertically in the water column, more or less standing on its head rooting out a morsel of food, with its head down in the muck, often with mud swirling around its head and eyes so that its vision is severely reduced. Many think that for this reason, tailing bonefish are the

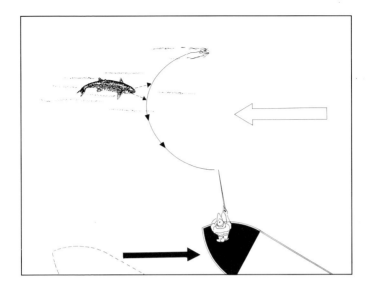

Correct Presentation and Retrieve — the fly is presented at the far side of the fish, and then retrieved so that as it approaches the front of the fish, it imitates the behavior of a prey making a sweeping turn to escape.

easiest to catch. But I take an opposite view. I believe tailing fish can be quite difficult to catch! Because they are so exposed, they are even more wary about danger. And, you must throw the fly close enough for them to see it, but not so close that they will spook.

Two options are open to you in this situation. One is to make the cast while the fish is rooting around down on the bottom. But to do this properly, *you need to understand which direction the fish is facing.* If you throw at the rear of the fish, chances are it will never see your fly. Usually a fly presented at a distance of about 18 inches from the fish's head is about right. The standard bonefish retrieve should be made in short two to six-inch strips or so, so that the fly hops naturally — across and in front of the bonefish.

The other option is simply to be very, very patient. You'll find that usually a tailing bonefish will tail, move a few feet, tail again, and so on. Be sure to note the direction in which the fish is moving and cast your fly six or eight feet ahead of that direction and allow it to lie on the bottom. The next time the fish ceases tailing, begins swimming forward, and is nearing the fly, begin the same standard retrieve.

Another very common bonefishing situation is to spot fish in water so shallow that their backs are either just under the surface or maybe even partially exposed. These fish will often meander around in just mere inches of

When casting to a tailing bonefish, or one with its back out of the water, make sure you know in which direction the fish is facing.

water, nosing into the turtle grass and coral trying to locate morsels of food. Bonefish in this environment are perhaps the easiest ones of all to alarm with noisy wading or a poor cast. The softest cast you can make (the sideways-and-up-cast I described earlier) is really ideal for this situation. I also prefer to work fish like this with flies no larger than #4, dressed with a pretty heavy or fluffy wing, which softens the fly's impact as it parachutes to the surface. Try to drop the fly at least eight feet ahead of the direction in which you think the fish is moving. Remember, your fly should always be presented so that it will not approach the fish from behind or at an angle.

The majority of bonefish presentations are to a fish that is approaching you from directly ahead, or at a slight angle. In such cases, if the water is more than about a foot deep, the fly can simply be dropped seven to 10 feet ahead of the fish and allowed to sink to the bottom. When the fish is within two feet of the fly, make two or three strips on the line, which will cause the fly to leap about 10 inches or so. Then allow the fly to sink to the bottom again. If the fish moves in, make a few standard six-inch strips on the line. If the fish follows the fly, but doesn't seem interested, make one or two long, very fast pulls. Hopefully, this will cause the fish to think your fly is trying to escape, and it will attack.

A cardinal rule for retrieving any fly is that if any fish closely follows for more than six feet and fails to strike, change the retrieve. Speed it up. Slow it down. Or if the fly is heavily weighted, allow it to drop to the bottom. This is a rule you want to live by!

Another situation that may be encountered is when a school of bonefish is moving in front of you. Sometimes the school will be moving quite rapidly, and maybe even demonstrating a fair amount of spookiness. The worst thing you can do is to simply drop your fly into that mass of fish. For if one bonefish spooks, they will all spook! A better technique is to cast your fly in front of the school as it approaches, and as soon as the first fish reaches the vicinity of your fly, begin the standard retrieve I have previously described. *But many times I have found that in these moving-school situations, making long and fast strips works best.* When this alternative stripping technique is successful, it is probably because the bonefish think a prey is trying to escape from the entire school.

A question I am frequently asked by beginning bonefish anglers is, why is it, even though I am making good presentations, and am sure bonefish are taking their flies, I am missing so many hook-ups? There is one reason for this, I think, and if you will learn the following tip, it may do more to assist you in hooking bonefish than any other retrieving advice I can give you.

Here's what is happening. The bonefish follows the fly, and you see its head dip down toward the fly. At that point you either feel nothing, or just a light tap — or a series of taps — on the line. Usually when its head dips down, the fish has grabbed the fly, and it most certainly has if you feel those taps. Yet, you continue to retrieve. And as the fish surges forward with the fly resting in its mouth, the forward momentum of the fish increases the forward motion of the fly — even faster then your retrieving motion — placing some slack in your leader and sweeping the fly forward and away from the fish.

To overcome this problem, as you are making your strips, *if you see the bonefish dip down its head as if it is going to take the fly, make two or three* long, slow *drawing pulls on the line.* To make this type strip, grasp the line in front of your hip and make a long, slow draw until your arm is extended behind you.

Such a series of long, slow pulls tends to keep the line tight and a hook-up generally results. I can't emphasize too strongly how marvelously this little trick will help you increase your score on hook-ups.

How to set the hook when a bonefish accepts your offering is something many anglers don't understand. If hooks are sharp, the strike is a very subtle thing. A bonefish doesn't slam into a fly like a snook or barracuda does. Instead, it tilts its head downward and *sucks* the fly into its mouth. When that occurs, the angler will feel just a very light tautness on the line. There is seldom ever any type of hard jerk.

When that happens, the *instinctive* way is the *wrong* way to set the hook when a bonefish accepts your fly. That is, the angler feels that the fish has taken his fly, and he sweeps his rod toward the sky. But, by striking vertically, if the fish wasn't hooked, the fly is going to be removed from the water and if the bonefish is nearby, the angler is

Incorrect Way to Strike Bonefish — Vertical Lift

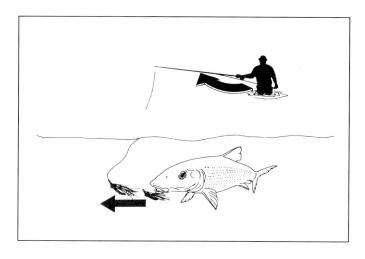

A Correct Way to Strike Bonefish — Side Strike

forced to make another cast so close to the fish that it will probably alarm it.

There are two recommended methods of striking any fish when it is in shallow water less than two feet deep. One is the strip strike, which means that the hand holding the line makes a slow draw backwards, which will bury the hook. The other method is to side strike, moving the rod to the side and parallel to the water. Either of these methods is more than enough to set the hook. And with either of these striking methods, (unlike the vertical rod strike), should the fish be missed, the fly leaps only a few inches away from the fish and is still underwater and close enough to the fish for another retrieve.

But if the hook is set, be ready for an explosive reaction from the bonefish. Usually, the fish will bolt away in what at first experience is an awesome run of great speed. Few people when they first hook a bonefish can believe that something that small can go that fast — but it can.

LANDING AND RELEASING FISH

When a bonefish runs, the classic rod position pose is to hold the rod as high above the head as possible. On a flat with a clean floor — such as white sand— there is no need for this. The overhead pose is needed only when you need to hold the line as high as possible to avoid a line cut when the fish is running over a flat encrusted in line-cutting coral and debris.

Allow the fish to make its first wild run against a lightly adjusted drag, then begin bringing the fish in. Chances are the bonefish will make two or sometimes three long runs, which will evaporate most of its energy. Just be patient and allow the runs to exhaust the fish, and you can land most bonefish easily, unless the leader or line snags on too much grass or is cut by coral.

When the fish is very close to you and ready to be handled, use the rod to lift its head out of the water. Once its head is above the surface, the only action a fish can take is to push more of its body above the water. Then when you feel the bonefish is tired enough to be landed, reel down until a portion of your leader is inside the rod guides, but be ready to release line if the fish surges away. With the leader inside the guides, you can lift the head from the water and slide the fish towards you. Trying to grab a fish while holding on to the lower end of a typical 9-foot saltwater rod can be difficult. But if you slide your hand up near the stripping guide — shortening the rod length — you will find it surprisingly easy to pick up the fish.

A large bonefish can easily be lifted with the comfort lift, which was developed in Australia. Slide your hand under the center of the fish's weight — not necessarily its length — and lift. If the fish slides to the left, simply slip the fish back into the water and slide your hand a little to the left. When your hand is in the center of the fish's weight, you can lift the fish and it will simply drape motionless over your hand.

I always use barbless hooks when seeking bonefish. I can't remember a time that I lost a bonefish because I was using barbless hooks. There are two advantages to this, as I see it. One, it is certainly easier to remove the hook. Second, and even more importantly, since bonefish will frequently escape capture through a leader cut on coral or a line snarl, a barbless hook insures that the fly will soon fall free of the fish.

When finally landed, many bonefish have exhausted so much energy that they may die if the hook is removed and they are simply turned free. There is one method of

Flip Pallot holding a bonefish upside-down so it won't move.

reviving any small fish that works best of all. If the fish has no sharp teeth — and bonefish don't have any teeth at all — firmly grasp the lower lip of the fish and its tail. Sweep the fish backwards in the water about a foot or so. Do this a number of times. When this is done, the backward motion causes the fish's gills to flare open and water is flushed over them. It is the life-giving oxygen that the fish needs, and using this method forces the maximum amount of oxygen over the gills. If you'll use this method of reviving fish, even if your fish is in poor condition, it will generally revive just fine and be swimming off to safety in just a few minutes.

Incidentally, never release an exhausted bonefish when there are sharks or barracudas nearby. Run off the predators before releasing the fish. Or even better, if the tide is high, take the fish to mangroves and free it in the flooded root system where it won't be vulnerable to attack while it's in a weakened condition.

OVERLEAF: *A happy angler with a 13-pound permit caught off the coast of southern Belize.*

CHAPTER FOUR

TECHNIQUES FOR PERMIT

The single most important element for catching permit on the fly is to have numerous opportunities to cast to them. Since you are always going to get a high rate of refusal, it behooves the angler to get as many chances as possible. *Successfully catching permit on a fly is generally a team effort, requiring a top-flight guide who knows how to locate the fish and put the angler in position to cast to the fish; and an angler with the skill to present the fly, make the proper retrieve, hook the fish, and fight it to the boat.*

LOCATING AND APPROACHING FISH

Just about all permit are caught while fishing from a boat, as permit are generally found in water deeper than you would wade for bonefish. The best depths average from 2 1/2 to 5 feet. Also, in most situations, exceptionally high spring tides are the best water conditions for finding permit. Isolated flats near deep water are prime places to look for them. As the tide drops, permit will drift into channels or deep water. But, as the tide begins to rise, they will cruise the perimeter of the flats, looking for crabs. Two excellent places to search on such a flat are at its oceanside where the tide is rushing in, and at its rear where the water is spilling off; as drifting crabs and other morsels that are tasty to permit tend to be concentrated in these two kinds of areas.

If there is a cold spell that drops water temperatures, small isolated flats adjacent to deep water are the most alluring places to permit, just as they are to bonefish. In fact, during such a cold spell permit can frequently be found there when they aren't visible anywhere else. Again, as I explained earlier, the reason for this is that deeper water does not become chilled like the water surrounding swallow flats. This same principle applies in the summer, when such flats are cooled with water from the depths with each incoming tide.

Another choice place to locate permit is along the drop-off of a flat bordering a channel. The fish will frequent these places, looking for food that is drifting or moving off the flat to the depths. Channels or basins that hold water eight to 12 feet deep with a bottom containing white sand holes are also excellent places. Permit will frequently suspend in these holes. And because this white sand contrasts so well with the fish, it is easier to spot them against such a background. Large flats, some one-square mile long or more, will hold permit too, if the depth on such a flat during high-tide stages exceeds two or three feet. The water surrounding bridge piers is another prime location.

Experienced fishermen know that you don't search for fish and expect to see a full profile of a fish under the water. Instead you may see just the suggestion of the fish.

Fortunately, with permit, there are some other indicators.

Remember, first, that almost all of a permit's body appears to be silvery, except the back and tail. This silver body will reflect the area over which the permit is swimming. A permit swimming over dark grass will look very dark, and one moving over white sand is almost all white. The black coloration on a permit runs from the head all the way to the upper and lower tail. If a permit is facing you, this distinctive dark back and tail may be the easiest part of the fish to see as you are looking down. Or if the fish is sideways to your position, you may also often see a thin black line and a wisp of a black "Y" shape — its tail.

Permit are also called floaters. That is, they often suspend just a few feet below the surface. Or like basking sailfish, many times — especially if the water is calm — they will suspend just under the surface, apparently resting. So you should concentrate your vision on these areas of the water column. Frequently you will see a tiny dark tip — maybe two — of either the dorsal or the tail fin protruding above the surface as the fish lie there resting. Years ago with my son, Larry, I entered the interior lake of the Marquesas Keys. There were so many fins and tails of resting permit and tarpon protruding above the surface of the lake that it appeared like a series of picket fences — a thrilling sight!

Permit are also called flashers. These are fish that roll sideways in the current, producing a flash of light similar to that of a mirror wobbling back and forth.

No one seems to know what they are eating, but permit sometimes appear to be sipping or nymphing on the surface of the water. They will rise, take some unseen thing from the surface, and then drop back underneath the surface. Rising fish exhibiting this behavior can often be seen from a surprisingly long distance.

Presentation of the fly to permit is critical to success. Slick, calm surfaces in shallow water offer perhaps the most difficult conditions, as permit seem to be more easily frightened by a splash on the surface than almost all other flats' species. Steve Huff, who guides Del Brown to almost all his permit catches — and is regarded by many as one of the best guides in the Florida Keys — says, "You gotta show the permit the fly. You need to drop it two or three feet in front of the fish when you can." This is one reason why Del Brown's Permit Fly is superior to the epoxy and other heavily weighted flies. It has a much quieter entry in the water at such a close distance.

The exact spot where the fly should be dropped differs with conditions. In shallow water, if the fish is cruising toward you, or is located at a right angle, the fly should be dropped as quietly as possible, no more than five feet in front of the fish. If the fish is holding in swift current under a bridge, along a drop-off of a flat, or other similar situations, the angler should position himself off to one side. And since from this position the current flow will push against the line and drag the fly sideways, the angler should cast slightly beyond the permit and upstream from it. Then the fly will be approaching the fish as if the current were bringing a morsel of food to it.

If you have located several fish, it is vital that you work to the fish on your side of the school. Never allow your fly line to fall over a permit, or it will surely flush.

At the completion of your cast, when the fly hits the water, lower the rod tip near the surface. Allow the fly to sink briefly and then begin a retrieve, which should be a series of three to six-inch strips on the line. Such a retrieve

Joe Brooks with a nice permit caught on the fly. Joe was one of America's pioneers in the development of saltwater flats fishing.

should be maintained until the fish indicates somehow that it has seen the fly. Usually it will move toward it. Anytime the fish surges toward the fly, stop retrieving and allow the fly to fall quickly toward the bottom. In water less than four feet deep, allow the fly to lie on the floor of the flat. If the fish pursues it and then turns off, begin the short series of strips again. If the fish turns toward the fly, allow it to sink again. Anytime the permit moves toward the fly, allow it to drop, just as a live crab would under similar circumstances. If the permit begins swimming away and you believe it will not again come to the fly, instantly make a quiet pick-up and cast in front of the fish and repeat the operation. *So long as the fish doesn't spook, keep repeating this technique.*

Many permit take a fly and eject it without the angler ever being aware that anything has happened. To avoid this, whenever a permit dips down, or alters its swimming attitude so that it is moving toward the fly, make a long slow draw on the fly line. This will keep the line tight, aiding the angler in determining if and when the fish has taken the fly. Even though a permit's mouth is relatively tough and leathery, a sharp hook will penetrate it easily, often resulting in a successful hook-up.

If you are fishing a Clouser Deep Minnow (which in very calm conditions can often be superior to a crab pattern, since it is thinner and makes a more silent entry into the water), a different retrieving technique should be employed. With this fly, you want to make an agitated retrieve, so that it is constantly diving and darting in very short motions, like a dancer who just stepped on a porcupine. To obtain this result, make a constant series of short, jerky strips as you retrieve line, twitching the rod tip slightly and frequently. Sometimes permit simply go crazy over the white-and-chartreuse Clouser pattern when it is retrieved in this manner.

For years we believed that permit did not take flies and that to catch one was simply blind luck. But, in the past several years people like Del Brown and Steve Huff have proven that with the right fly and the proper presentation

Del Brown with a permit caught in the Florida Keys.

and retrieve, permit will definitely take flies. As proof of that, Del and Steve recently fished the lower Keys and in two days caught 10 permit on a fly. That is not luck!

OVERLEAF: *Lefty releasing a giant tarpon, Florida Keys.*

CHAPTER FIVE

TACKLE AND TECHNIQUES FOR TARPON

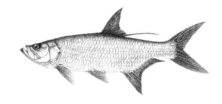

TACKLE

Tackle for tarpon varies greatly, simply because fly fisher-men seek this species in a wide range of sizes from as small as 10 inches to as large as 200 pounds or more. So perhaps it would helpful in evaluating tackle for tarpon to divide tarpon angling into three size categories: tarpon from 10 inches long up to a maximum weight of, say, 20 pounds (which I define as small tarpon); tarpon from 20 pounds to about 50 or 60 pounds (baby tarpon); and the giant tarpon, those weighing 60 pounds or more. Within the giant tarpon category, it is even possible to argue for a fourth size category for fish weighing over 150 pounds, as monsters of this size may require unusually large and powerful fly fishing tackle.

Rods

In fishing for *small tarpon*, a typical bonefish rod, that is, a 9-foot rod for a 7 or 8-weight line, is ample.

For *baby tarpon and most giant tarpon* you will encounter, rods need to be a bit stouter. A 10-weight rod is ideal for almost all of this fishing. Some fly fishermen use a 12 or 13-weight rod on tarpon weighing from 60 to 140 pounds — this has been the conventional thinking for more than a decade. But for baby and giant tarpon — certainly those weighing up to 140 pounds or so — there are several flaws with this technique, in my opinion, and I disagree with it. First of all, people who really are not serious fly fishermen, but who enjoy going once a year or so with a guide, find that these very heavy rods and lines are much too cumbersome for them to handle. A number of fly fishermen have told me they gave up tarpon fishing because they simply couldn't handle the big 12 and 13-weight rods and lines. And as you might imagine, since they lack the physical strength of men, most women generally have tremendous difficulty with such heavy tackle unless they have been able to spend considerable time mastering it.

These people would be far better off with a rod they can handle well. Because if you can't work the rod properly on the cast, you simply aren't going to perform well. But today, the modern 10-weight graphite rods — or, at the most, 11-weight rods — have extra strength concentrated in the butt, so that they are powerful enough to land fish of this size category.

I have landed a number of tarpon up to 136 pounds on a modern 10-weight rod with its reinforced lower portion. Because for this type fishing, the important consideration about rod size is not so much how strong the rod is for the task of fighting the fish, but rather, how well it can lift weight. Because once the fish is tired and brought to the boat, it often has to be physically lifted with the rod into a position where the guide can lip-gaff or release it. If the

Ed Given, of Salinas, California, holding in his hands proof that lifting a big tarpon can break a fly rod. But why do you suppose he's smiling?

lower portion of a fly rod is not well reinforced, that is when the rod will break — on the lift.

But with proper technique, that is, by using the butt of the rod to fight and lift the fish (which I'll discuss in more

OVERLEAF: *Billy Pate fighting a tarpon in the Florida Keys.*

detail later in the book), even relatively light rods will allow you to subdue surprisingly large fish.

For fish that weigh from 150 pounds or more, slightly larger tackle is suggested. These giants will require a really powerful rod for the lifting chore, such as a 12 or 13-weight model. Such rods have incredibly powerful butt sections and can lift enormous weights.

Rod length for giant tarpon is a personal choice. I favor 8 1/2 feet in length, but many giant tarpon anglers prefer rods 9 feet long, or infrequently even longer. Since it is rare that you will ever be casting to a tarpon at a distance of more than 65 feet — and most tarpon presentations are much closer than that — I think an 8 1/2-foot rod is long enough to perform well when casting at these distances. And after the hook-up, the shorter rod offers several advantages: it puts more leverage on the fish during the fight; it is easier to pump and wind with; and at the end of the battle after you have caught this huge fish, it is easier to handle during the stressful time when you and your guide are trying to get rid of the fish! For all of these reasons I feel an 8 1/2-foot rod is the ideal compromise when fighting giant tarpon or any very large fish.

Larger tarpon rods are often equipped with a foregrip — frequently referred to as a fighting grip — located between the rod handle and the first stripping guide. Some tarpon fishermen feel a fighting grip is useless and should not be installed on the rod. I don't agree.

Those who object to having a fighting grip on a tarpon rod feel that by placing their hand that far up on the rod blank, they lose much of the lifting power of the rod. Their reasoning is as follows: since the rod bends only from the point where your hand grips it, if you grab the rod at the first stripping guide and attempt to pump the fish, the rod will bend very little below the stripping guide. But move your hand down to the fighting grip and a more powerful portion of the rod comes into play. But then go even one step further: remove the fighting grip and grab the rod even further down the blank — at the upper end of the handle — and now you are using the full power of the rod blank to pull against the fish.

And certainly by gripping the rod at the upper end of the handle you can use the heaviest portion of the rod to fight the fish. But, those who advocate this concept are excellent tarpon fishermen who can routinely land 100-pound tarpon in 15 minutes or less.

Unfortunately, most fly fishermen who go after giant tarpon only once or twice a year do not possess the polished skills of these anglers, and it takes them a considerably longer time to subdue a tarpon of any size. For such anglers, who will spend a half an hour or more battling even a baby tarpon (something that is usual rather than unusual), the fighting grip can be a godsend on the really big ones. Because even though it may be better technique for applying maximum pressure to fight the fish by gripping the rod blank at the upper end of the handle, this is a rather uncomfortable way to hold the rod. After an extended period of time fighting a fish by gripping the handle, the average fisherman is likely to become very tired and even begin to experience muscle spasms or cramping in his hand and forearm. At this time, he can grasp the fighting grip and fight the fish while his hand and arm rest a bit. When you consider that the fighting grip on a rod shouldn't normally spoil the casting action of the rod in any manner — because that is principally determined by the design of the rod tip — I think it makes good sense to use a rod equipped with one.

Today's best tarpon rods cast and fight well. Twenty years ago, we fished with rods that were so stiff you could

Lefty lifting a giant tarpon caught at Homosassa, Florida, several years before it became known as a giant tarpon destination. To the right is Harold LeMaster, who fished this area for years without telling anyone of his fabulous discovery.

pole a canoe with them. You could certainly fight fish with them, but they were the very devil to cast. Beware of such rods that are stiff as a poker throughout their length. If you ever get the fly to the fish, a stiff rod will certainly do the job. But catching a tarpon means you have to first make a good presentation, and that means having a rod tip that will flex enough to load and throw the line. So it's more effective and easier for the average tarpon fisherman to use a rod designed with a powerful butt section that tapers gradually so that the rod tip is rather soft, allowing him to cast the line with the tip for a decent presentation.

Reels

Reels for small tarpon can be those that possess only a light drag, and many freshwater models are good for this. Small tarpon almost never make a run of more than 30 yards and usually much less than that. They expend their energy by jumping and soon are subdued. For such fishing, any reel with a little drag is fine.

For baby tarpon, you may sometimes encounter fish that will take even as much as your fly line plus 100 yards of backing, although that doesn't occur too often. A reel that holds 200 yards of line should be ample for almost any situation you will encounter in fishing for baby tarpon. But, you do need a reel that has a smooth drag with which you can maintain at least a pound of straight-pull drag pressure on the reel.

When fly fishing for all giant tarpon, I favor a reel that holds, in addition to the fly line, a minimum of 250 yards of 30-pound backing. Reels that hold more line than this usually have a larger diameter spool, which permits the angler to recover more line faster as he turns the reel spool. This is one reason that for giant tarpon, some anglers prefer the very large reel models normally used in fly fishing for sailfish. Such reels as the Abel #5, a John Emery, an Islander #4, or a Billy Pate Marlin reel, are models that I frequently see being used.

Lines for Sight Fishing — Lines for sighted fly fishing to small and baby tarpon can be standard or conventional weight-forward tapers. They work fine. But for giant tarpon, most anglers use various special purpose lines.

The conventional method for sighted fly fishing for giant tarpon in shallow, clear water is to stake out or anchor the flats' boat in a place where the tarpon are known to travel and wait for them to approach. Most often one person — normally a guide — mans the poling platform at the stern of the boat, while his companion, the angler, stands on the casting platform in a ready position. This is visual fishing, so that the angler and guide will normally see the fish before a cast is made.

When a tarpon is located, most anglers will wait until they can clearly see the fish before presenting the fly. Since rarely is the cast to a giant tarpon more than 60 feet, and because heavy rods are employed, special lines have been formulated for this type fishing. They are actually modified weight-forward tapers. Most of them have a stiffer running line at the rear to reduce tangling when line is shot. The heads are rather short and fat, designed with very short front and back tapers. These lines — which you might say are sort of overgrown Bonefish Tapers — are designated, obviously, as Tarpon Tapers.

Two densities of line are used for giant tarpon fishing in clear shallow water: floating or slow-sinking. For inexperienced giant tarpon anglers, the floating line may be their most effective instrument, since it can be picked up easily from the water for the back cast.

But floating lines have three major disadvantages. First, if there is floating grass on the water — and this is a frequent occurrence on the flats — as the fly is retrieved the floating line will capture grass that will travel down the line to the leader and spoil the presentation (whereas slow-sinking lines will usually slip through grass and drop below the surface).

Second, floating lines will not permit the fly to sink deeply into the water column, where in many instances the tarpon may be swimming.

And third, floating lines are always thicker in diameter than slow-sinking lines, so that when it is necessary to throw into a stiff breeze — which is, of course, a frequent occurrence on the flats — it is considerably easier to deliver the fly with a slow-sinking line that has less wind resistance than a floating line.

But slow-sinking lines have disadvantages too. For example, a slow-sinking line may sink too deeply if the cast is made too soon; and because of water tension, it simply can't be lifted out of the water quickly if a hasty back cast is required; but must first be retrieved to a level where the angler can lift it easily from the surface for another cast. But despite these drawbacks, many experienced tarpon fishermen prefer the slow-sinking line.

There are two basic slow-sinking lines. One is the conventional fly line which has been designed to sink slowly. You can purchase them in a variety of densities with sink rates from very slow to very fast. For example, a conventional very slow-sinking line that is quite popular is one designated as Intermediate.

Another popular line for giant tarpon is the Monocore line, originally developed for tarpon fishing, which sinks a bit faster than the Intermediate line. It is a clear monofilament line with a strong core of nylon, making the line virtually invisible in the water, a decided asset if an improper cast has been made, since tarpon frequently won't flare away from an underwater Monocore line —

whereas they might spook from a brightly colored line.

Perhaps the best line rig for giant tarpon fly fishing is a line which combines a front portion of slow-sinking Monocore — which is nearly invisible and doesn't spook tarpon — with a rear portion of a floating line that can be picked up quickly and silently. What some very sharp guides in the Florida Keys are doing is combining the good points of both types of line. Here's what they do: they cut off the first 6 feet of the front taper of a floating Tarpon Taper line and replace it with 6 feet of 60-pound mono-filament. To this they then attach a basic giant tarpon leader — usually 6 to 10 feet in length. What this results in is a line that has an entire front section of 12 to 16 feet of clear and practically invisible monofilament. But, the rest of the line floats, and thus can be picked up fairly easily for a back cast.

Or, if you don't want to build your own, Orvis now markets a line with similar specifications. Their fly line designers have attached 10 feet of commercial Monocore to a floating Tarpon Taper. It is a superb connection, and, in my view, is the best compromise for a line to fly fish for giant tarpon in clear shallow water.

Either the modified line made by guides in the Keys, or the Orvis design, provides another benefit. Because the rear of the line floats, the angler can toss the fly slightly in front of the tarpon and allow it to sit there for a brief period, since the floating line will hold the fly near the surface. As the tarpon approaches the fly, the retrieve can then be made. If the first fish in a passing school refuses the fly, a pause in retrieve can be made until another fish is in position and the retrieve can then be continued.

Billy Pate fighting a tarpon in the Florida Keys.▶

Lines for Blind Fishing — In the Keys, Florida's west coast, Homosassa, Belize, and several other top tarpon habitats, you can see tarpon clearly in water less than 10 feet deep. But, when you fish in deeper water (often 25 feet or more in depth) or where the water is muddy, or where fish are in deep channels or holes, or in jungle rivers, such as in northeastern Costa Rica, tarpon are rarely seen, except when they roll on the surface. In these situations, you will be blind fishing, and you will need to get the fly down deep to the fish's level in the water column.

For this type fishing, a different type of line is required. For many years the preferred line for this type angling was a lead-core shooting taper, which permitted the angler to cast great distances and benefit from the super sinking characteristics of lead.

Another superb tool now available for this work is the Teeny Nymph line. The T-300, T-400, and T-500 lines — the fastest-sinking designs in the Teeny series — have a long, heavy belly section that is level throughout its length. Attached to the rear of this sinking section is a floating line. The Teeny lines will sink almost as fast as a lead-core shooting taper, but provide the advantage of a more easily handled floating line behind the head. Also gaining popularity these days is the Scientific Anglers' Uniform-Sinking line, which has a belly section and front taper constructed of the same diameter, so that the front taper will sink just as rapidly as the belly section to position the fly deeper in the water column.

Because of their thin diameters and high densities, all of these lines cast extremely well, permitting the angler to make longer casts than would normally be possible with a conventional floating or slow-sinking line; and they sink rapidly to provide a longer search with the fly throughout the water column.

Leaders

Leaders for tarpon differ from those for bonefish and permit. The major difference being that tarpon, even some of the small ones, have abrasive mouths that will abrade a light tippet that would not normally be damaged by a permit or bonefish. To prevent this, a section of heavier leader should be attached in front of the more fragile regular tippet. This section is traditionally referred to as a "shock tippet," but I prefer to use a more accurate description, referring to it instead as a "bite tippet."

For small tarpon weighing from four to 20 pounds or so, a 9-foot tapered leader with a bite tippet of 20 to 30-pound monofilament is suggested.

For baby tarpon, up to 60 pounds, usually a tapered leader is not employed. Instead, a 4-foot straight butt section of at least 30 to 40-pound monofilament is generally used. However, if you encounter baby tarpon that appear to be especially spooky, it is often advisable to lengthen the butt section considerably. For example, when fish are swimming over white sand, or are "laid up" — just resting beneath a calm surface — a butt section as

Tapered Tarpon Leader. At top is shown a standard tapered leader comprised of a butt section, a mid-section, and a tippet. For tarpon, as shown at bottom, a heavier section of monofilament bite tippet should be added.

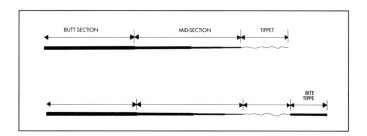

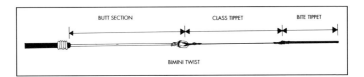

Basic Baby and Giant Tarpon Leader. This leader is comprised of three parts: a butt section of 30 to 40-pound monofilament, a class tippet (tied generally with a doubled Bimini Twist), and a bite tippet of 60 up to 200-pound monofilament, depending upon the size of the tarpon you are angling for.

long as 12 to 16 feet may sometimes be called for. To this butt section a length of class tippet — usually about a 15-inch length of 12 to 20-pound monofilament — is next added. Finally, to this class tippet should be tied a short length of 60 or 80-pound bite tippet. If you are seeking a world record or to maintain your eligibility to compete in many of the popular tarpon tournaments, you must use a class tippet at least 15 inches long, together with a bite tippet no less than 12 inches long.

The same leader that is used for baby tarpon is employed for giant tarpon — fish weighing from 60 to 180 pounds. For these fish, generally an 80 to 120-pound clear monofilament bite tippet is suggested. But, for very large fish, those weighing 180 or more pounds — and who can really mangle a piece of monofilament — a 200-pound bite tippet may even be called for.

Some people use bite tippets of wire (braided or solid trolling wire), but generally have poor results. My experience dictates that clear monofilament is much to be preferred over wire for bite tippets on tarpon.

For presentations deep in the water column, leaders should be simple and as short as possible. Long leaders tend not to sink as fast as the line, and if you use a leader exceeding 6 feet, the fly will always be higher in the water column. Many people who are fishing 12, 16, or 20-pound class tippets will loop the back end of the Bimini Twist class tippet directly to the line and add the 80 to 200-pound monofilament bite leader on the front end.

Flies

Tarpon flies, just like lines, can be divided into two types. One type is designed to be fished in clear and relatively shallow waters. The other is tailored for deep-water fishing, where the tarpon can't be seen.

Clear-Water Flies — Flies for clear-water fishing have several basic design characteristics that differ from those used in deep water. Clear-water flies are generally shorter (although not always) and are made from soft, supple materials (marabou, rabbit fur, soft hackles, etc.), that undulate with every twitch on the line. They sink relatively slowly and can vary in color or combinations of color.

Clear-water tarpon flies can be divided into two categories: 1) small tarpon flies, for use on tarpon weighing up to about 20 pounds; and 2) baby and giant tarpon flies, for use on tarpon weighing from 20 to 180 pounds.

The same basic design can be used for all clear-water tarpon flies. The wing of the fly is almost always attached at the rear of the fly. If chicken hackles are used, then I recommend neck hackles instead of saddle hackles, as neck hackles are wider and present a more visible profile in the water. The hackles are tied in splayed fashion, so that the legs work like a swimming frog. About three to four hackles are positioned on each side. The length of the wing hackle extending behind the hook bend is almost never longer than an adult's ring finger, and often only as long as the little finger. A few patterns will be dressed with

Clear-Water Small Tarpon Flies: Top row, left to right, *Popping Bug and Cactus Fly;* bottom row, *Examples of how marabou is tied in a Keys' tarpon fly style.*

mylar or other reflective materials (Crystal Flash, Flash-abou, and so on), but most are devoid of flash. Marabou is often used, particularly on smaller flies, since it gives off a lot of action with little twitching of the line. Also, it tends to suspend the fly in the water column because of the air that gets trapped in its fibers, permitting the angler to make a slower retrieve — an advantage when fishing for small or baby tarpon in very shallow water.

Directly in front of the wing are usually wound one to three neck or saddle hackles. These are then laid back and down, so they point toward the wing, and the thread is wrapped over these. This laying back of the hackles accomplishes several desirable things. It adds a bit of color to the fly (almost all of nature's creatures are not of a uniform color); it makes it easier to cast the fly; and to

Clear-Water Baby and Giant Tarpon Flies: Top row, left to right, *Popping Bug, Chinese Claw, Cockroach;* bottom row, left to right: *Blue Death, Tarpon Bunny, Red and White, Black Death.*

some degree, laid-back hackles, if properly tied, prevent the wing from underwrapping on the hook shank and spoiling a presentation.

Deep-Water Flies — What revolutionized deep-water tarpon fishing was the development of specialized sinking fly lines and unique fly patterns for deep-water fishing. Visibility down deep is restricted, but tarpon are nevertheless very sensitive to objects moving through the water. That's the key to deep-water tarpon fly design. These flies are designed so that they create water turbulence as they swim on the drift or retrieve. This is accomplished by constructing the fly with a very bulky body and wing.

There are a number of available patterns to choose from. A typical and successful — and my most favorite — tarpon pattern for deep and dirty-water situations is the

Deep and Dirty-Water Tarpon Flies: top row, *White Whistler;* bottom row, left to right, *Black/Orange Whistler and Yellow/ Red Whistler.*

Whistler series, developed by famed saltwater fly fisherman, Dan Blanton, of San Jose, California. Such flies usually consist of a body constructed of large-diameter chenille, with lots of bucktail tied around the shank, and often with an underwrapping of lead wire. In front of the chenille are secured widely splayed, stiff neck hackles that flare to give maximum resistance to the water. Large bead-chain or lead eyes are positioned just back of the hook eye, and a bulky head is often formed by winding chenille around the eyes. This design results in an incredibly bulky fly that "pushes" water, giving off vibrations that tarpon can sense. Black or dark-colored patterns are usually the most effective. In fact, in low-visibility or dirty water, darker colors almost always out-perform any other color combinations. But, the combination of red and white or yellow and red also seems to do very well.

When fished with a lead-core shooting taper, Teeny Nymph line, or Uniform-Sinking line, Whistler patterns will fish well at depths down as far as 25 or 30 feet if the current is not too stiff, provided you employ the proper drift or retrieving techniques, which we will discuss later.

If the water is dark, dingy, or roiled with mud (as is the case in many jungle rivers) then darker-colored patterns are often the best fly choice. However, even in these situations, yellow and red, or red and white, still do well.

TECHNIQUES

Many of the fly-fishing technique suggestions made for fishing bonefish and permit on the flats also apply to the third great fish in the flats' trophy category, the tarpon, whether they be two or 200 pounds. However, the feeding behavior and, of course, the sheer size of tarpon, dictate some special techniques that we want to investigate.

Small Tarpon Techniques

You will recall that we separated tarpon into three categories: small tarpon, baby tarpon, and giant tarpon. Small tarpon are fished for somewhat differently than baby and giant tarpon, one of the reasons being that small-tarpon habitat is somewhat different than that of its bigger cousins. Small tarpon can be found on saltwater flats, of course, but they generally prefer to exist in small canals, estuaries, and lagoons.

One way to locate any tarpon, including the small ones, is to look for rolling fish. Perhaps more tarpon have been located initially by seeing them rolling than any other method. Under good light conditions, rolling tarpon in a size of over 10 pounds or so can be seen on a calm surface

Tarpon rolling

at a distance of a half mile. This rolling behavior is a consequence of the tarpon's ability to obtain oxygen from air as well as water. The tarpon is one of the very few species of fish that can do this. That is one of the reasons that small tarpon can survive in small and shallow bodies of water which do not contain sufficient oxygen to support many other species of fish.

Once seen, a rolling tarpon is never forgotten. As a tarpon rolls, the surface is broken and the top of the body moves up and over in a humping motion.

Rolling tarpon fool many anglers, who will cast where the fish rolled. But when tarpon are in water more than five feet deep, they will frequently move up to the surface, gulp in a breath of air, and dive straight back to the bottom. Other times the fish will definitely be moving in a particular direction as they roll. But fortunately for us, their course is rather predictable.

If possible, when you see tarpon moving along and rolling, try to quietly motor well ahead of them, and then simply stop the motor and wait for them to come to you. Thousands of tarpon have been caught using this technique. If the fish roll in deep water and don't seem to be moving, notice the direction in which they roll. If they come up, roll, and dive in one particular direction, cast about 10 to 15 feet ahead of the direction of the roll and allow the fly to sink deep, because many times these rolling fish are following a routine of lying on the bottom, coming up for air, and then returning to the bottom.

One of the most exciting types of tarpon fishing for me is to engage small tarpon — weighing from about five to 20 pounds — with a light 8-weight rod loaded with a floating line with a 9-foot tapered leader and a bite tippet of 30 or 40-pound monofilament. And, one of the best times to enjoy such small tarpon fishing occurs on exceptionally strong spring high tides, when the mangrove roots are flooded with 18 inches to three feet of water. Pole along the edges and look for these small tarpon. They frequently will suspend in the water among or just outside the roots of the mangroves. Usually they are motionless or swimming very slowly.

Here, I recommend using a fly made from marabou or neck hackles that provide a lot of movement to the short wing. It is tied in similar fashion to any fly used in clear-water tarpon fishing, dressed on a #1 or #1/0 hook. When the fish is located (sometimes you have to look very closely to see the dark green fish among the dark mangrove roots) cast so that the fly lands a foot to 18 inches in front of the fish. Try to make as soft and subtle a cast as possible. Slow-swim the fly past the tarpon. You'll almost always get an instant strike. But, be forewarned that you're likely to lose quite a few of these fish because of the obstruction of the mangrove roots. So, try to move the fish away from these roots and out to open water. Also — even though again you'll be losing some fish in this situation — I recommend using barbless hooks.

The same flies and tackle discussed above can also be used on small tarpon that are known to hold or can be seen rolling in deeper waters — sloughs, lagoons, or deep canals. But there are times when a small popping bug (the size should be geared to the size of the fish being caught) is the most effective offering you can make to these fish.

Also, small tarpon can frequently be found on bonefish flats — especially on the higher stages of a tide — resting or holding in white sand holes surrounded by turtle grass. When you encounter this type of situation, move your boat from one light sand hole to another, dropping small flies in the holes as you go along. I have often found that popping bugs — no matter how small — won't work here, as they often spook fish. So, a silent streamer is decidedly better. Try to stay back from the hole and make the longest and quietest cast you possibly can. One of the best places for this type fishing is in Belize.

Baby and Giant Tarpon Techniques

Clear-Water Techniques — If you are new at the sport, you will find that when fishing for these larger tarpon you will be surprised at how small a fly a 125-pound tarpon will take. Baby and giant tarpon can be fished in clear water with flies that have a wing length of no more than 2 1/2 inches. For many years anglers fished with #5/0 hooks, then moved down to flies dressed on #4/0 hooks. Today, many experienced guides and fishermen prefer that their giant tarpon flies be dressed on #3/0 hooks — and a few very successful anglers are using flies even as small as those dressed on a #2/0 hook. Some guides feel that stainless hooks are too soft. Instead, they prefer carbon steel hooks, which are stronger. I have had good results with both types of hooks. It's a personal choice, I suppose, but there's no denying that carbon steel hooks will hold a point better than those of stainless steel.

What is important is how the hooks are sharpened. Considering the mouth of a tarpon, you'll need a well-supported point that will drive into very hard material. This means sharpening the point so that it is either triangular shaped or diamond pointed. Either method will give you a well-supported point that has cutting edges along the sides to aid in penetrating the hard mouth of a tarpon. Some guides will snip about 1/16 of an inch from the hook point prior to sharpening. They feel that this makes a stubbier point that will not collapse on contact.

Once tarpon grow somewhat larger than 20 pounds, their behavior changes. They are usually found in a different habitat than the very small fish. Baby and giant tarpon prefer more open water, deep channels, and wide and fairly deep basins where they can feed on crabs, mullet, pinfish, and the larger food sources that are not of interest to small tarpon. Baby and giant tarpon roll just like small tarpon, and can be located the same way, though bear in

Looking into a Giant Tarpon's Mouth

mind that there are exceptions. I have seen tarpon of 100 pounds or more working through a murky flat in water so shallow that their backs protruded above the surface like a green checkerboard. But to locate large tarpon — especially those exceeding 50 pounds — you will generally find them in water exceeding four feet, and often in water 12 feet or more in depth. Therefore, they must be fished for somewhat differently than the small ones.

Very early and late in the day, tarpon will often do what fishermen refer to as "laying up." They will rise to a position just below the surface and suspend there. It can be a single fish, but more often there will be small schools of them. Many times you will find them by seeing just a portion of the dorsal fins sticking above the surface. Such fish are exciting to see, but beware that they can be very easily frightened. A silent approach and a very subtle cast, made with a leader at least 12 feet long that lands the fly softly no more than three feet in front of the fish, are mandatory presentation techniques.

In the regions where tarpon exist, large resident tarpon will almost always be encountered throughout the entire year. These fish follow very regular patterns, and you can find them if you will observe daily tidal flows and search the flats to determine where the baitfish seem to be most plentiful, as that's where the tarpon will most likely be.

But in many parts of their range most tarpon are migratory: they will move into an area during certain periods of the year and then move on. For example, the migratory giant tarpon of the Florida Keys arrive in the Key West area sometime in January or February. They slowly move up through the backcountry for the next few months, then slowly work their way out toward the Atlantic Ocean side, and finally, sometime in July, they seem to disappear. Years ago, some shrimpers working the Gulf of Mexico

The dark blue line in the water is a school of migrating tarpon.

told me that in December and January they often saw huge schools of giant tarpon rolling on the surface. It seemed to these fishermen that the fish were coming from the direction of Mexico, heading toward the Florida Keys. But where tarpon come from and where they go is not certain. This lack of information is mainly due to the fact that tarpon are not regarded as a commercial food fish, so there has been no economic incentive to fund long-term scientific studies on the species.

Fortunately, large tarpon have some characteristics that help anglers find and fish for them successfully. When tarpon are cruising in an area, they generally keep to water from four to 12 feet deep. If there is an underwater obstruction, such as a rise in the bottom, they tend to follow such uprisings. The famed Buchanan Bank in the backcountry of Islamorada, in the Florida Keys, is a classic example of an uprising that forms a sort of underwater wall in a deep basin that large tarpon like to frequent. For many years Keys' guides have been staking out their boats along this bank.

Anytime you can find tarpon cruising in an area of deep water with an underwater point that rises several feet to a depth of six to 12 feet of water, you have found yourself a hot spot. Anchor at the end of the point. The tarpon cruising along will encounter the point that extends out into deep water, follow it to the end, and then make a turn — giving you a good shot at them. Such an underwater point is especially productive if it is covered in white sand. Big tarpon cruising over white sand stand out like a coffee stain on a wedding gown.

Once you find tarpon and are in position, you need to get ready. As explained earlier, strip off line, remove the coils, make a false cast, and re-establish your line properly on the deck. When the tarpon approach, make a cast so that the fly lands a few feet in front of the school. *Don't cast to the whole school, but to a single fish.* This is a basic mistake made by most fly fishermen new to the tarpon game. Throwing at a school of tarpon is just like shooting at a flock of quail. Any experienced hunter knows that you'll bag more birds by selecting a specific quail to shoot at. The same goes for tarpon. It's best to cast to the lead fish. If that fish ignores the fly, there is a chance that a tarpon behind the first one will take it. Try never to cast over the backs of fish. Only put the leader and fly in front of fish — never the line.

You will also occasionally encounter what tarpon fishermen refer to as a "daisy chain" — a group of large tarpon swimming in a tight circle, usually in shallow water.

It is not good technique to cast your fly into the middle of a daisy chain. The impact of the leader or line will probably spook the fish. Sometimes with a long leader, or when using a Monocore fly line, you can get away with it.

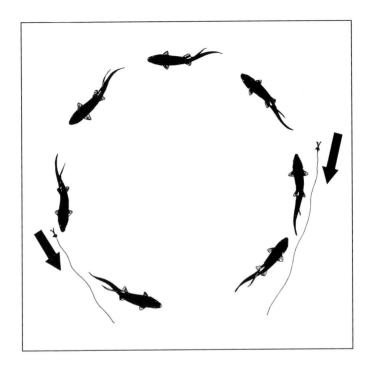

A "Daisy Chain" of Tarpon

But you really do need to throw on the correct side of the circle. If the tarpon are moving in a clockwise manner, and you are at a six-o'clock position to the fish, never throw the fly at nine o'clock. The fish coming around the circle will see the retrieved fly swimming straight at them — in the attack position — and I think you should be keenly aware by now that I don't advocate presenting the fly so that it appears to be attacking the fish! Instead, cast the fly at two or three o'clock, and as the fish come around

OVERLEAF: *Saltwater offers its own special moments of serenity. Sunset at Ascension Bay, Yucatan, Mexico.*

the circle they'll see the fly swimming away from them, imitating natural prey behavior.

Just as in bonefishing and permit fishing, be very much aware of where the fly lands. The basic retrieve for tarpon is a series of slow strips about a foot long. If a fish loses interest, change the method of retrieving. But high-speed retrieving is usually not effective on tarpon. If at all possible, you want to be able to watch the fish as well as the fly. *It is vital that you know the position of the fly,* or you will have no idea what the fish is doing. If you are watching the fly you will see when the fish takes it.

Now that you are watching the fly closely, *it's next in importance to understand how a tarpon takes the fly.* It doesn't snap it like a barracuda. Instead, it opens its big mouth and sucks in water, just like a vacuum cleaner would pick up a speck of dust.

How to strike a tarpon has been a never-ending discussion among tarpon fishermen. I have fished with many of the best, including Harry Kime — who I believe has probably caught twice as many giant tarpon as any other man in the world — and Bill Barnes, who runs Casa Mar, a tarpon fishing camp in Costa Rica, whose total on big tarpon has never even been counted. In their long fly-fishing careers, these and several other friends have landed literally several thousand tarpon! From their recollections and my own experience since the 1960s, I have formulated some techniques for striking tarpon that work well for me, and I recommend them.

First, never strike a tarpon by raising the rod — sometimes referred to as striking with the rod tip — as you would with many freshwater species, because the tip tends to collapse when you bring it back against a fish the size of a tarpon. A tarpon exceeding 60 pounds usually has a mouth much like the inside of a metal bucket. There are few places where a fly will sink into its flesh and bone. And you need to drive that hook home smartly and vigorously, and you simply cannot do it with a conventional vertical rod lift.

If you know where the fly is and you can see the fish inhale it, *wait until its mouth closes and then set the hook.* There is a much-repeated myth that you have to wait until the tarpon turns its head after gulping the fly. But many times the fish never does turn. It simply inhales the fly, and if you wait for the head to turn, you may see the fly expelled as the fish continues moving forward.

When the mouth closes, it is evident the fish has the fly. At that time, make a one-two-three count *before you strike. I think this slight delay is vital to consistent hook-ups. Striking too fast often means a missed fish.* I make a long, slow draw on the fly. When I feel definite resistance on the other end, that is the time to strike.

Bill Barnes, Nick Curcione, Harry Kime, and many other very fine tarpon anglers set the hook with what you might call an exaggerated or tarpon strip strike. It is the method I also use and suggest you do too, since it has served me and others so well. The butt of the rod is held against the body. Draw back on the line and hold it securely. When the tarpon feels the hook, it will usually rock its head back and forth, and if you are holding onto the line, this rocking action helps bury the hook in its mouth. *Make three or four sharp and VERY SHORT sweeps of the rod butt in a direction away from and to the side of the fish, while holding onto the line. These sweeps have to be short and they have to be made with* the rod butt, *not with the tip.* Use the body, not the rod, to strike a big tarpon. The rod butt should be tucked against the body. Then with the arms almost locked (never use the wrist to set the hook), and with the forearms holding the rod level with

Look what a giant tarpon can do to a #4/0 hook!

the water, turn your body. This allows you to set the hook deeply with all the combined power of your legs, back, and locked arms.

What is vital is that the moment the fish begins its escape run, you want to do *no more striking*. What breaks a leader is a jerk on it. A running fish, with the angler continuing to set the hook, creates a distinct chance of jerking on the fragile leader and breaking it. Let the fish make the first wild run.

I prefer to fish my tarpon using a light drag, never more than a pound of direct pull from the reel. By cupping the fingers against the inside of the reel spool, I can apply additional drag pressure if I need it. And, I'll have the line running through the fingers of the hand gripping the rod, so I can trap the line there for additional pressure. Either the fingers inside the reel or those that are trapping the line against the rod can be released instantly if I choose. I prefer this method to a higher drag setting. Some very fine tarpon fishermen do well with a higher drag setting, but for me, using this lower setting reduces my chances of a sudden leader-breaking jerk.

Once the tarpon is hooked and begins its escape, you should forget the tarpon momentarily and remember that the biggest source of trouble may come from the loose line between the reel and the stripping guide. You should do several things the instant the hook is set and the fish begins to run. First, form an "O" ring around the loose line with your fingers. This is used to control and feed the line being pulled by the fish to the guides. It allows you to get the line out from under your feet, off the deck, and so on.

The hand holding the rod also is working at the same time. Tuck the rod handle flush against the forearm and turn the reel so that it is away from you and the forearm is between you and the rod and reel. This prevents the line from snagging on the reel or end of the rod. As the final bit of loose line approaches the rod (with your fingers forming an "O" ring to control it) bring the "O" ring to a position near the rod about half way between the stripping guide and the reel. If you bring it to the rod too close to the reel, it may snag around the reel and come too close to the stripping guide, over-wrapping the guide and snapping the leader. Once all the loose line is funneled through the guides, the rod can be brought down and into a normal fighting position.

If a knot appears in the line lying on the deck as the fish escapes, you have one option that may save you. The knot will usually bind, not in the first or second guide, but up in a snake guide of the tip section where the rod is deeply bent. This is because when the rod bends, the line will be taut against the snake guides. As the knot arrives in the tip section, it will not follow the rod but leap from guide to guide. It is here that the knot can bind against the wire of one of the snake guides. *If you see a knot approaching*

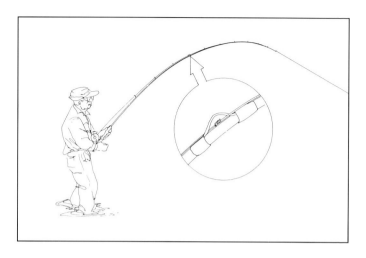

Turn Rod Upside-Down

the stripping guide, turn the rod upside-down and the line will be forced to flow along the rod blank and not bind on the guides. If the knot is too big, it won't be able to squeeze hrough, but more than half the time what would be a leader-breaking incident, for sure, is averted by turning the rod upside-down.

Tarpon jump. Oh how they jump! It's one of the elements that endears us to this great gamefish. But if the fish jumps and the line is taut, there is a good chance that the leader may break. So, there is a need to throw slack while the tarpon is in the air. But, as soon as the fish goes back in the water, pressure must be applied against the fish.

There are two commonly used methods of getting that desirable slack while the fish is above the surface. One is to bow to the fish. As the fish rises, make more or less of a bowing motion and push your rod toward the fish. Be careful not to push it too hard, as this may create unwanted slack that may cause the line to wrap around the

An unusual photograph of Lefty playing a tarpon from the bank at Casa Mar, Costa Rica. A deep channel in the jungle stream runs just a few feet from shore.

rod tip or the head of the tarpon, resulting in a line break.

Another method of getting slack, which I prefer when possible, is to dip the rod. As the fish rises above the surface, simply dip your rod toward the fish, so that the tip actually penetrates the surface of the water a few inches. This will create controlled slack that prevents the line from wrapping on the rod tip or around the fish.

Only experience will teach you how much pressure to apply on a tarpon. One thing that will help is to string up a rod at home and attach the fly line to a sturdy object to see how much pull and what amount of jerking will break

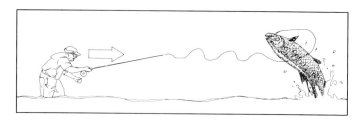

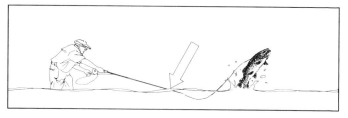

Bowing (top) and Dipping (bottom) Rod to Leaping Tarpon

the leader, so you'll know how far you can go before the leader breaks in an actual fishing situation. What you really want to do is apply as much pressure as you dare without breaking the leader. Remember, what generally breaks the leader is not a hard pull, but a sudden jerk. Try to keep all jerks on the leader from happening. *And also remember, anytime the fish surges away, drop your rod and point it at the fish!* This rod attitude presents the least amount of drag pressure. Once the fish completes its surge and resumes a normal swimming pattern, you can slowly bring the rod back up into a fighting position.

As I apply pressure on a big tarpon, I like to keep the rod low, almost parallel with the surface. I think this is much better than fighting from an overhead rod angle. Almost all fishermen I observe move the rod through far too much of an arc when they pump. If the rod butt is raised too much above 45 degrees, the actual pressure on the fish decreases.

To check this out, you can conduct a simple experiment that may be enlightening. Hook a scale to the leader end and have someone trap the line against the rod and begin to raise it. At first the scale will indicate an increase in pressure. But as the rod passes above and beyond a 45-degree angle, pressure begins to drop off; and when the rod reaches a vertical position, you'll note that rod pressure rapidly decreases.

What you want to do is make short pumps, recovering line each time. Using the butt of the rod is the way to fight big, strong fish. Just as you don't strike big fish with the rod tip, you don't fight them with the tip either.

When a big tarpon is brought within 40 feet or less of the boat, vertical rod pressure should not be used, except in the final moments when the fish is to be lifted to the surface to be boated. *Use side pressure instead.* This is accomplished by keeping the rod very low to the surface and to the side. What is most important when doing this is that the rod should be pulling the fish off balance. For example, if the fish is moving left of the angler, the rod should be lowered to the right. This tends to pull the fish off balance and causes it to work harder.

Dan Blanton, an old angling friend and great tarpon angler, explains it this way: "If you hook a mule to a wagon and put the wagon directly behind the mule, the mule can exert the maximum pull on the wagon with the least effort. But place the wagon off to one side and the mule is pulled off balance and has to work much harder to move the wagon". It's the same with a tarpon.

When tarpon are close to the boat and becoming exhausted, they will frequently try to get to the surface and gulp in energy-giving oxygen. If you can prevent them from doing this you can shorten the fight. This can be accomplished by watching the fish. If it looks like it is trying to raise its head above water to inhale oxygen into its mouth, place your rod down low — even underwater if necessary — and try to pull the fish down and over. This technique, developed more than 30 years ago in the Keys, can shorten the fight immeasurably.

When you finally have the fish at boatside, you face the considerable task of hauling out of water as deep as six feet below you a live and violent animal that may weigh 100 pounds or more. This is the very reason why tarpon rods are so stout, since you need the lifting power of the butt section to raise the fish into a position where the guide can grab it.

When the fish is lifted to boatside, you can use a gloved hand to grasp the tarpon. What most experienced anglers do — since almost all tarpon are being liberated these days — is to use a lip gaff, a short gaff with a sharp point but no barb. The point is inserted into the middle of the front lower lip of the fish, and then held securely by pinning the gaff point against the side of the boat. In this manner, even very large tarpon can be handled, so that the fly can be removed and the fish freed with a minimum amount of stress to the animal.

Deep-Water Techniques — When fishing in deep or dirty water where tarpon can't be seen, the techniques for striking and fighting the fish are virtually the same as clearwater techniques, provided, of course, you feel the fish has taken your fly. But, retrieving the fly in deep water is another matter altogether.

In a river or tidal deep-water situation where the water is moving well (and assuming you are using a sinking line and fly), the best retrieve is the "do-nothing" retrieve, or a drift. After you have cast the fly across the current and allowed it to sink as deeply as possible, simply hold the line and let the current do the work for you by vibrating the fly during its drift below and behind the boat. Occasionally, you can make a series of slow, foot-long strips of the fly line to bring it nearer to the boat. This generally changes the elevation of the fly in the water column as it lofts toward the boat. Then, the fly line can be slowly played out again and allowed to drift in the current.

For many years, this has been the best single retrieving technique for tarpon where there is a current and sinking flies and lines are used.

But, in areas where there is no current, the fly should be cast out and allowed to sink as deep as it can go. Then long, slow one-foot retrieves should be made.

INDEX

FLY FISHING FOR BONEFISH, PERMIT & TARPON

Designed by Grits Morris and Robin McDonald.

Color Photography by:
Andy Anderson (page 36)
R. Valentine Atkinson/Frontiers (pages 10, 16, 17, 27, 78, 118/119, 127, 144/145)
Lefty Kreh (pages 2, 21, 23, 44/45, 114)
Brian O'Keefe (pages 32, 106)

Illustrated by Rod Walinchus, Livingston, Montana.

Text composed in Berkeley Old Style by Compos-it, Montgomery, Alabama.

Film prepared by Compos-it, Montgomery, Alabama.

Color separations by Photographics, Birmingham, Alabama.

Printed and Bound by Arcata Graphics Company, Kingsport, Tennessee.

Text sheets are acid-free Warren Flo Book by S.D. Warren Company, a division of Scott Paper Company, Boston, Massachusetts.

Endleaves are Rainbow Antique.

Cover cloth is by Holliston, Kingsport, Tennessee.